UnCommoditized

Uncommon Ideas for Commoditized Markets

Saikat Dey &
Gerrit Reepmeyer

Contents

Acknowledgments

We would like to thank several corporations and individuals whose contributions have been invaluable in creating this body of work.

We would like to begin by thanking McKinsey & Co., our alma mater, who believed in our endeavor to understand and decode the world of commodities and actively supported us in our mission. The contributions of D.J. Johnson, Mei Mei Hu, Conway Tang, Joe Hughes, and Rob Latoff were particularly noteworthy. They were our partners-in-crime and actively supported this effort through their research, analytical efforts, and overall mentorship and guidance. The body of knowledge of this topic would not have been in its current shape, if not for their contributions.

We would also like to thank the multiple corporations and the individuals who we have worked with while at McKinsey & Co. for providing us feedback and validating our findings. While we cannot name these corporations or individuals for confidentiality reasons, please know that we are grateful for your help.

Moreover, we would like to thank Aleksey Mordashov, Vadim Larin, and the Severstal family for giving us their trust and confidence to implement some of the findings in this book at Severstal North America. As they say, the proof of a good strategy is in its implementation, and it is the Severstal family and its leadership who provided us with the canvas to paint our thoughts on.

In addition, we would like to thank the following colleagues and friends for providing valuable contributions for editing this book: Steve Tatum, Jo Isenberg, Vipul Amin, Gayatri Chandrasekharan, and Professor Oliver Gassmann.

Lastly, we would like to thank our colleagues at Ockham Razor, Mikhail Zhavoronkov and Anupam Sengupta, as well as our families, who endured several days and weeks of "unresponsive behavior" while we were trying to put all these pieces together.

Our experience shows that writing a book is a team sport, and we are eternally grateful to the team mentioned above and the innumerable people who aren't mentioned here who helped us make this a reality.

Saikat Dey
Gerrit Reepmeyer

Preface

During late 2014 and early 2015, numerous people have asked us, "What's going on with the price of crude oil? It used to be $100 per barrel just six months ago, and now it is $50 per barrel. Will this price be permanent? Should I buy some forward contracts?" Unfortunately, commodities like crude oil or steel usually get all the attention only when prices are either very high or very low. However, all this attention also indicates one critical fact: Commodities and cyclical industries are fundamental pillars of our economy.

Many people, including managers, CEOs, and investors, have always thought of commodity markets as something that is difficult to understand and they often stay away from it. Many people even raise the question, "Why should I pick a career in a commodity industry that is not glamorous, lacks innovation, and depends on many exogenous factors that are nearly impossible to influence?" Our response has often been, "Because it's fun. We believe commodity markets represent some of the toughest challenges in management. Yet, not many industries offer what cyclical commodities can offer by bringing it back to the basics: The ability to win through basic economics combined with business acumen and disciplined execution."

The following example illustrates what we mean: How many of us have a preference for the brand of gasoline that we fill in our cars? Gasoline is a true commodity product and is priced closely across various vendors within a certain neighborhood. Most people, therefore, choose a gas station based on its location, such as its proximity to their homes or the side of the road they're driving on,

Performance
Share price development[1]
Indexed
(Jan. 2000 = 100)

1 Share price adjusted for dividends and splits

Fig. 1. ExxonMobil significantly outperformed other major oil and gas companies over the past 15 years (examples: ExxonMobil, BP, and Shell).

but less on the price or brand of the gasoline itself (BP, Shell, or ExxonMobil). Yet, some oil and gas companies consistently outperform others in markets where brand differentiation and customer preferences do not seem important, and in addition, pricing of the product is highly cyclical.

Let's consider Figure 1. Over the last 15 years, ExxonMobil has outperformed BP and Shell by over $100 billion in market capitalization, delivering superior shareholder value despite the recent challenges in the price of crude oil. Upon a closer look, ExxonMobil did it not just because it has a better brand, operational discipline, or a dedicated workforce, but because ExxonMobil has a clear and disciplined approach to the commodity cycle.

The ExxonMobil case is one of many examples in commodity markets where some companies are outperforming others, even though these markets do not allow differentiating products based on just brand or price. This book picks up on this phenomenon and attempts to answer the fundamental question: Why do some companies outperform their competitors in relatively undifferentiated and commoditized product markets?

This book builds its answers on easy-to-understand micro-economic concepts and industry case examples; it concludes with a comprehensive cycle management framework that can be applied to any cyclical commodity market and similar industries.

About the Authors

Saikat Dey is a co-founder and the CEO of Ockham Razor Ventures. Previously, Saikat served as the CEO of Severstal North America, which was a subsidiary of OAO Severstal, a global metals and mining company, employing 2500 people and considered one of the best examples of the heavy manufacturing revival in the United States, with flagship locations in Michigan and Mississippi. Saikat led the successful divestiture of these assets in September 2014 to AK Steel and Steel Dynamics for $2.3 billion.

Saikat joined Severstal from McKinsey & Company where he served as an Associate Principal in the Global Energy and Materials practice. He is recognized as a thought leader on investment strategies, commercial optimization and operational improvement within the metals and mining industries. Prior to McKinsey, Saikat held positions at IBM and a number of early-stage technology companies in various sales and product marketing roles. He holds an MBA from the Tuck School of Business at Dartmouth and an undergraduate degree in Mining Engineering from the National Institute of Technology in India.

Gerrit Reepmeyer is a co-founder of Ockham Razor Ventures. Prior to that, Gerrit was Vice President, Procurement at Severstal North America, managing $3.5 billion in annual spending across iron ore, coal, scrap, metallics, and energy from a supply base of nearly 3000 vendors. Before joining Severstal, Gerrit worked with the energy company E.ON in Germany as a Principal in the company's In-house Consulting group.

Gerrit joined E.ON from McKinsey & Company where he was involved in numerous projects advising Fortune 500 companies primarily in the industrials and energy markets. Gerrit was part of the team developing the firm's knowledge around cyclical commodity markets. Prior to McKinsey, Gerrit worked with an early-stage venture capital firm in New York. He holds a Master's degree in business and engineering from the Technical University of Berlin as well as a Doctor in Business Administration from the University of St. Gallen in Switzerland.

I. Commodities and Cyclical Industries: Why They Matter

Cyclical commodity industries are a major part of the global economy. By definition, commodity industries include any industry that offers basic and primary products that are not very easily differentiable. Examples include agricultural products, oil and gas, cement, energy, metals and mining, chemical, pulp and paper, and many others. To illustrate the nature of a commodity product, think about an energy company trying to sell electricity. Electricity is nothing else but electrons flowing through a cable. The consumers have no preference—and in most cases do not even know—who is producing the electrons that they consume. How can an energy company therefore effectively differentiate itself against its competitors?

In addition, commodity products are typically used by companies that engage in producing manufactured goods, such as automobile companies using steel to produce cars, or food and beverage companies using agricultural products to produce groceries.

According to Figure 2, commodity-related industries are estimated to be directly responsible for 24 percent of global GDP and indirectly for another 31 percent of global GDP via industries that are consumers of commodities, such as manufacturing, automotive, or food processing industries. This translates to 55 percent of global GDP that is directly or indirectly affected by characteristics and behaviors of commodity markets. What all commodity markets have in common is the fact that they exhibit high degrees of cyclicality, meaning pricing can

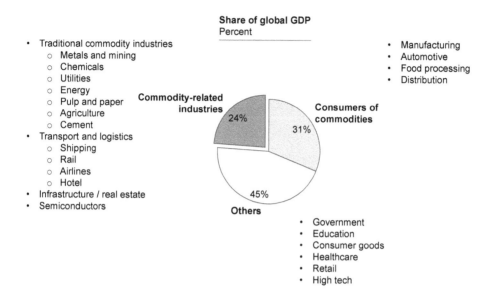

Fig. 2. Cyclical commodity markets are a major part of global GDP.
Source: Estimates based on Global Insight data.

fluctuate significantly. We will discuss the concept of cyclicality later on in more detail.

Given their importance for global GDP, the question arises: How can cyclical commodity industries be characterized and what is special about them?

One answer that describes cyclical commodities is that—at first sight— they seem to be difficult markets, and therefore, many people consider them unattractive. For instance, most shareholders and investors regard cyclicality as a negative phenomenon, given the limited predictability of future cash flows. Also, young management talent has traditionally overlooked commodity businesses as a preferred place to start and build a career. The number of cyclical commodity companies listed as the most preferred employer for young graduates is very humbling.

Truthfully, cyclical commodity industries face many challenges that other industries might not face. Table 1 provides a summary of the most typical environments that every commodity company faces and what it means for the attractiveness of the business.

Table 1. Typical Environment of Commodity Businesses and What it Means for their Industry Attractiveness.

Typical Environment of Commodity Businesses	Examples	What it Means
Infrastructure and equipment are highly capital intensive	A steel plant can cost $1.5 to 5 billion; refineries can easily cost $4-5 billion	It can take 10+ years to see a return on investment
Demand grows on average with GDP	Demand for steel grows in line with worldwide GDP growth; white paper demand has been shrinking, replaced by ebooks/Internet	Revenue streams are unstable and unpredictable; growth rates are typically low
Pricing is highly volatile	A barrel of crude oil has fluctuated between $53 and $107 within 2014; a difference of more than 100 percent between peak and trough in just 1 year	Costs are difficult to predict and do not necessarily correlate with revenues
Margins are thin and can be negative for many years	Integrated steel companies in the United States on average have not generated positive net income margins between 2009 and 2013	Companies can face several years of negative margins; putting entire industries at the verge of bankruptcy
Products can hardly be differentiated	Power companies sell electrons; the consumer has no preference – or does not even know – who is producing the electrons	Products are interchangeable and companies have limited incentives for innovation

The right hand column in Table 1 can be summarized as follows: You have to invest several billions of dollars to be able to produce your product, your market grows with GDP at best, your sales price and cost structure is highly unpredictable, you can barely differentiate your product, and you might have to wait for more than a decade to see a return on your investment. Does this sound like an attractive business environment to you? While many people would intuitively answer "No," our answer is "Yes!" This book will explain why.

As the ExxonMobil example in the Preface pointed out, cyclical industries also allow for tremendous opportunity. Figure 3 shows examples of companies in different commodity industries that were able to generate substantial value for their shareholders above and beyond what some of their direct competitors were able to generate, even though they were active in the same commodity markets and exposed to the same pricing at the same time.

Total return to shareholders[1]
Annualized, Percent

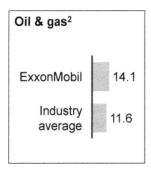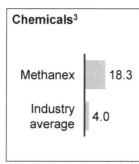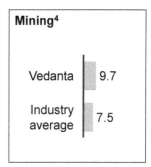

1 Annualized, historical total return to shareholders (TRS), simple average
2 Calculated over multiple cycles; 1994-2008
3 Calculated over 2000-2008 cycle (across 1994-2008 cycle, TRS: Methanex 3.1% vs. industry average of 2.8%)
4 Calculated over one cycle; 2003-08

Fig. 3. Across many different commodity industries, some companies were able to significantly outperform others.

For example, ExxonMobil delivered an annualized total return to shareholders (TRS) of 14.1 percent throughout the last couple of full commodity cycles in oil and gas which was from 1994 to 2008, whereas the industry average delivered only 11.6 percent. This allowed ExxonMobil to generate $100 billion more in shareholder value above and beyond what the average of their competitors was able to generate over the same time period. Even more extreme, Methanex—a United States-based methanol producer—was able to outperform its industry by more than 4× in terms of shareholder returns. In mining, the company Vedanta has shown a significantly better performance than its industry peers, with an average TRS of 9.7 percent over the last respective cycle compared to 7.5 percent for the mining industry as an average.

In addition to the examples of publicly listed companies, there are further examples of highly successful companies in cyclical commodity markets, such as Koch Industries or Cargill, the two largest privately held companies in the United States. Koch Industries is a conglomerate that is active in industries such as fuels, chemicals, fibers, plastics, pulp and paper, and fertilizers. All its businesses together generate revenues in excess of $120 billion per year. Cargill is active in agricultural commodities, energy, steel, transportation, production of feed, and food ingredients for application in processed foods and industrial use. All of Cargill's businesses generate approximately $140 billion in revenues per year. While public numbers about profitability are not available, both the Cargill family as well as the Koch brothers, Charles and David, are well known to be among the wealthiest families in the United States.

When looking at shareholder value created by successful companies such as ExxonMobil, Methanex, Vedanta, Koch Industries, or Cargill, it can easily be argued that many factors in cyclical commodity markets are exogenous to the realm of influence of managers. This could include structural issues, such as substantial over- or under-capacity in a supply market, external shocks that drive demand up or down, or unforeseen changes in the regulatory environment. While those external occurrences have a significant importance to any business, they set the same boundary conditions for every company in a certain industry.

This means the following: Despite the challenges of cyclical commodity markets and despite the fact that all commodity-related companies are exposed to the same exogenous, environmental conditions, such as commodity pricing or industry structure, there are many examples of well-performing companies that are able to outperform their direct competitors. This book attempts to explain why the successful companies have been successful. It will focus on all areas that can actively be influenced by management. Based on the strategies used by successful companies, this book concludes with a framework that can be applied by anyone in any cyclical commodity industry.

In summary, the business environment faced by cyclical commodity businesses represents probably one of the most difficult challenges that any manager can face. Therefore, anyone who is excited to solve some of the toughest problems in business and to understand how to unlock value from cyclical markets is encouraged to continue reading this book!

II.   The Cost Curve: The Key to the World of Commodities

To decode the world of commodities and to understand how to unlock value from cyclical markets, there is one predominant topic that managers need to understand: The industry cost curve which is also known as the supply curve. Mastering the concept of the cost curve in all its facets and applying it in the right context will provide managers with the most powerful tool to decipher how commodities behave.

Let us try to understand the cost curve in more detail: In its simplest form, the cost curve is a representation of all the producers of a certain commodity organized in ascending order of their cash cost to produce a unit of that commodity on one axis (y-axis) with their total production capacity per plant represented on the other axis (x-axis). The cash cost per unit for each producer is ideally calculated using all cash costs incurred in the production (e.g., raw material cost, conversion cost, labor cost, utilities, transportation/delivery cost, interest cost) divided by the total production volume of the plant. Cash costs do not include items like depreciation or amortization. Consider the hypothetical graphic in Figure 4 which represents the industry that produces a mythical commodity "*Unobtainium.*"

The cost curve in Figure 4 tells us the following:

(1) There are seven producers of "*Unobtainium*" – namely Circle, Square, Rectangle, Pentagon, Sphere, Triangle, and Rhombus.

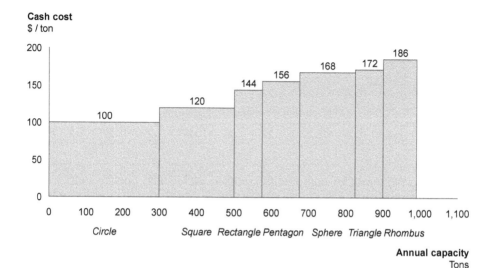

Fig. 4. Schematic illustration of a cost curve in a commodity market.

(2) The producer with the largest capacity is Circle with 300 tons of capacity while Rectangle and Triangle have the smallest capacity of 75 tons each.

(3) The total production capacity of the entire industry is ~1000 tons/year.

(4) The cash cost to produce 1 ton of "*Unobtainium*" varies from the lowest at $100/ton (Circle) to $186/ton which is Rhombus.

(5) The industry seems to be fairly consolidated with just three producers (Circle, Square, and Sphere) managing over 65 percent of total production capacity (~650 tons aggregated capacity in an industry with a total of ~1000 tons).

After understanding the supply side in a commodity industry (all producers and the cost at which they produce), the more interesting part becomes understanding the demand side. Just like a cost curve there is a demand curve, which, interestingly, is a lot more difficult to create. The y-axis of the demand curve exhibits the cash price per unit that the consumer is willing to pay. The x-axis of the demand curve describes their total need. Unfortunately, it is the y-axis where often demand curves fall apart as most customers never reveal or cannot quantify reasonably what the true value of the commodity they are consuming is to them. For example, it is easier for a gasoline company to tell you how much it takes to produce a gallon than for the consumer to quantify what is the maximum they are willing to pay for a gallon of gasoline.

Oftentimes when the demand curve is not well-documented, the most pragmatic way to represent demand is to illustrate it as a vertical line overlaying the cost curve (see Figure 5).

Building on the cost curve for *"Unobtainium"* that we just introduced, three new elements were added to Figure 5 compared to the previous version.

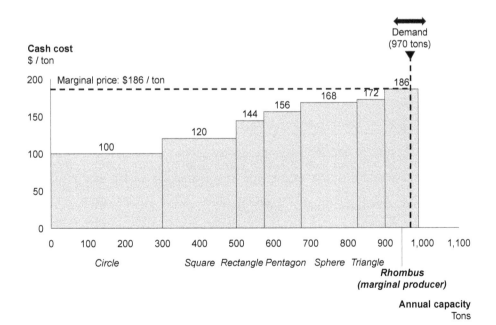

Fig. 5. Supply, demand, and price setting in a commodity market.

While you cannot determine what the true "value" for every consumer of "*Unobtainium*" is (i.e., the maximum price that they would be willing to pay for one unit), the total demand of "*Unobtainium*" in terms of number of units is typically known. When plotted against the x-axis (vertical line), it intersects the cost curve at the producer Rhombus whose cash cost for production is $186/ton. This makes Rhombus the marginal producer, which literally means that Rhombus is the last producer who can still break even on a cash-cost basis to fulfill overall demand in the market. And herein lies the fundamental economic concept of the price-setting mechanism in commodities. In most scenarios, the price is set by the cash cost of the marginal producer in the market and it often proves to be the long-term floor for the price of a commodity. Prices can often go above this price or below it for a period of time, but they typically settle back to this intersection point in the long term.

This new curve in Figure 5 also informs us of the following:

(1) Total demand in the market is 970 tons. This means that overall industry capacity utilization is rather high at 97 percent, which is calculated at demand of 970 tons divided by the total capacity of 1000 tons.

(2) Producers and the overall industry seem to be making very healthy cash margins. For example, Circle is making a cash margin of $86/ton (marginal price of $186/ton minus cash cost of $100/ton).

(3) If demand increased by more than 30 tons and no additional supply is introduced, then one would witness what is called "fly-up" pricing. This is a phenomenon wherein there is not enough capacity to serve the demand and pricing disconnects from the floor of marginal pricing. Customers will out-bid each other, fighting for overall existing supply in the market.

(4) However, if demand reduces by more than 70 tons, then pricing would fall by $14/ton to $172/ton (Triangle becomes the marginal producer). At this point, the industry has two choices: (i) Operate at full capacity forcing Rhombus to shut down at some point, or (ii) most players in the industry could take some capacity out of the market to retain Rhombus as the marginal producer and keep pricing at current levels.

(5) It is natural to expect at this point that Rhombus will try to reduce its cash cost to remain competitive, ultimately leading to the "*flattening*" of the shoulder of the cost curve.

As Figures 4 and 5 illustrate, cost curves are fascinating. They reveal a lot of valuable information about an entire industry. As a next step, let's apply some of these concepts to defining and understanding industry structure and behaviors. In the first case, we distinguish between a flat cost curve and a steep one and its implications. Let's look at a hypothetical industry called "*Chemex*."

In scenario A (Figure 6), the difference in cash cost between the lowest cost player and the highest cost player is only $11/oz which means that producers are fairly close to each other in terms of their production cost. Consequently, an industry in scenario A is very price-competitive and industry behavior must be all about winning volume. The more ounces each company can produce and sell, the greater the company's chances of survival will be.

Most processed commodity industries will eventually start to look like scenario A, given the very nature of competitive behavior and the industry's ability to shut down inefficient capacity. Being in an industry described in scenario A is not a great place to be. It's a "dog-eat-dog" world with very little returns for the capital that every player has invested. The only hope that usually sustains this industry is that at some point in time, there will be "fly-up" pricing which will make up for years of meager earnings, if any.

Scenario A: Flat cost curve

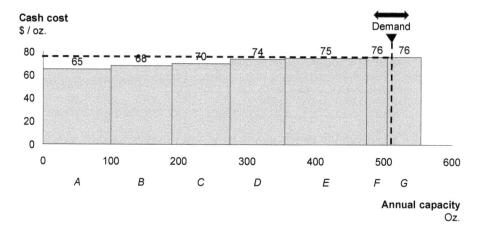

Fig. 6. Flat cost curve.

In scenario B (Figure 7) however, the difference in cash cost between the lowest cost player and the highest cost player is $95/oz. Most players are making healthy margins except for the marginal producer "G." This industry structure intrinsically faces two kinds of risks.

Scenario B: Steep cost curve

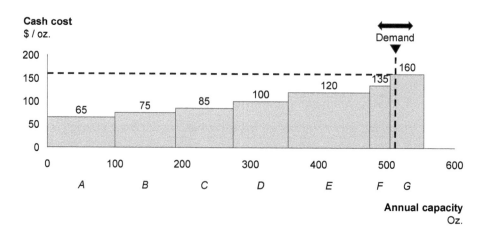

Fig. 7. Steep cost curve.

First, players do not understand the value of the marginal player (in this case "*G*") and often ask for its closure or push it into closure by turning up production beyond normal utilization numbers. If player *G* shuts down or will be pushed out of the market, the overall industry faces the risk of a price and margin reduction of $25/oz.

The second risk that an industry with a steep cost curve faces is new capacity additions. Higher profits often invite newer capacity and that always changes the supply/demand balance, leading to lower profits for the industry.

Another benefit of cost curves is their ability to help understand overall industry structure. Consider the two examples shown in Figure 8 and Figure 9.

In scenario C (Figure 8), we observe a highly fragmented market with over 26 individual players where no one player has a market share of more than 4 percent. In an industry which is structured in this manner the probability of good conduct is rather rare. Operating in this structure feels hypercompetitive and

Scenario C: Fragmented industry

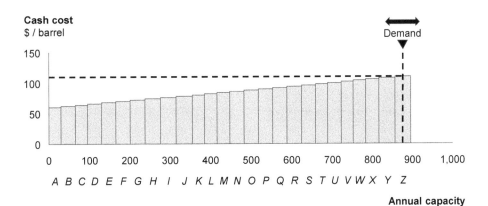

Fig. 8. Cost curve in a fragmented industry.

opens up the possibility of consolidation for someone with the right rationale and capital structure.

By contrast, scenario D (Figure 9) exhibits a market with only three players (*A*, *B*, and *C*), each having several production assets. On an aggregate level, each of the players holds a significant share of this highly concentrated market. In markets with a high degree of consolidation, pricing can rise well above the marginal producer threshold as players may have the capability and incentive to keep the supply/demand balance relatively tight. For example, one player may believe it would be more beneficial to take out production capacity in order to keep pricing higher. The net gain could exceed the cost of taking out production capacity. Only a player with the right capacity and the incentive can do this. This helps understand why highly consolidated markets typically raise more antitrust concerns than fragmented markets. We will talk in more detail later about an individual company's ability to influence industry behavior.

Scenario D: Consolidated industry

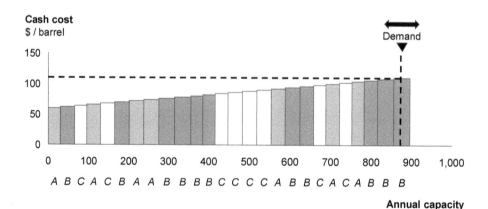

Fig. 9. Cost curve in a consolidated industry.

To conclude this chapter, let's recap some highlights:

- Cost curves are the most powerful tool for decoding the world of commodities.
- Cost curves describe industry supply and production costs. Therefore, they are a great framework to understand how long-term prices are set.
- The shape of the cost curve (flat or steep) reveals a lot about how individual companies are likely to act.
- Cost curves help understand overall industry structure (fragmented or consolidated) and, therefore, the market power that each player has.

In the next chapter, we will build on the cost curve concepts and apply them to commonly accepted beliefs in the industry, debunking some of the myths around commodity markets.

III. Applying Cost Curves to Challenge Commonly Accepted Beliefs

This chapter takes the concepts of the cost curve and applies them to commonly accepted beliefs in the real world. Some of the resulting insights might be surprising and not necessarily intuitive.

Belief #1: The High Cost Producer Needs to Shut Down

Belief #1 deals with the role of the high cost producer in a commodity market environment. Most often, one hears CEOs of large commodity manufacturers complain about the existence of high cost, inefficient producers who don't have the right to serve the customers they serve. It's not uncommon for a lot of remarks to sound like the following: "It's those high cost guys hanging around that's making this industry so competitive. If only they could get out of the market, we would not have the dog-eat-dog world we have out there."

Based on the framework of cost curves we just studied, let's try and understand if there is any merit to the kind of statements that are often made. Let's consider the cost curve in Figure 10.

In the example that we used in the previous chapter, Rhombus is the marginal producer and is barely staying afloat while the rest of the industry is making

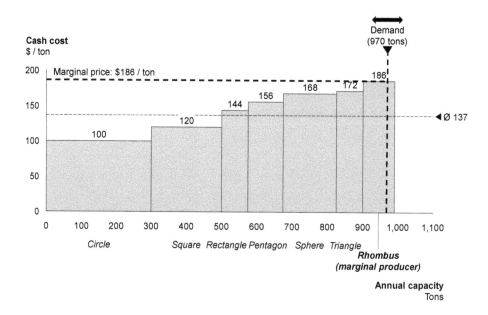

Fig. 10. Market economics of exemplary commodity market.

decent margins (with an average cost of $137/ton it translates to $49/ton of average cash margin for the industry).

Now, let's assume that Rhombus' ownership decides that it isn't worth staying in this business given their low returns and shuts down, and every other producer amps up production by 9% to make up this gap. In this scenario (see Figure 11), pricing falls by $14/ton for the entire market as Triangle becomes the marginal producer. As Rhombus disappears and Triangle takes its place, the average cash cost of the industry also falls by $5/ton (from $137/ton to $132/ ton). But that is not enough to make up for the $14/ton drop in pricing. Hence, the industry as a whole is worse off with Rhombus shutting down.

However, the answer is a lot more interesting for each individual player. Please refer to Figure 12 for the change in total margins for each player in each scenario. As you can see, the one player least impacted by this change is Circle and the one most impacted by this change is Triangle.

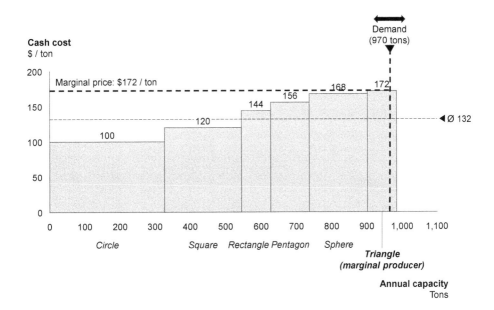

Fig. 11. Market economics after the marginal player has been taken out of the market.

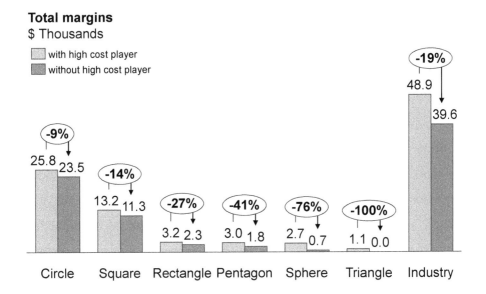

Fig. 12. Change in margin with and without a high cost player.

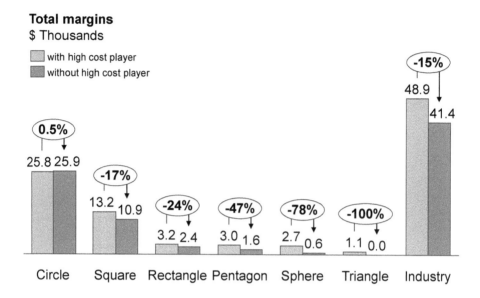

Fig. 13. Change in margin with and without a high cost player, assuming the Rhombus' production is backfilled by low cost players.

Now let's consider the scenario wherein Rhombus' production is backfilled only by the three low cost players in the following proportions: Circle (additional 60 tons), Square (additional 10 tons), and Rectangle (additional 10 tons). In that scenario, the change in margins is shown in Figure 13.

As you can see in Figure 13, the only entity that benefited from Rhombus shutting down was Circle while the rest of the industry suffered. While most producers want to be lean and efficient and on the left side of the cost curve, they lack appreciation and admiration for what the high cost producer provides in these markets—a high price and thus high margins. And so, while one individual producer may be motivated in increasing capacity and shutting down the high cost producer, they are usually doing this at the expense of the entire industry and potentially putting the industry in a flat cost curve environment which is very difficult to get out of in the long term.

Belief #2: Commodity Markets Don't Depend on Innovation

Belief #2 deals with the role of innovation in commodity industries. Innovation is typically something that does not come to the top of someone's mind as a potential value lever when people think of commodity-based industries, especially when compared with other sectors such as high tech, consumer electronics, or biotechnology. A lot of this is based in reality given how slow traditional commodity industries such as steel, cement, paper, and others have been in adopting new technologies, products, and processes. In fact, a colleague of ours had once presented information that stated that it took an average of 22 years for the steel industry to commercialize something from academic research while industries dependent on innovation as their key driver of value creation take only about 6 to 8 years.

The question arises that in an industry that is slow to adopt innovation, is this a critical determinant of success? Let's consider two examples: One from the natural gas industry and one from steelmaking.

Over the last few years, the United States has been the biggest benefactor of significantly increased access to natural gas reserves which was largely driven by the commercialization of shale gas, hydraulic fracturing (fracking), and horizontal drilling techniques. Let's understand how these events unfolded on the cost curve (see Figure 14).

As one can see in Figure 14, prior to the commercialization of fracking and horizontal drilling, the cost curve was primarily made up of assets that used conventional drilling methods. At that point, most of the shale gas reserves—even though already existent for many years—were out of the money and potentially could not be accessed economically. This led the industry to have a higher price point at the intersection of the demand and the supply curve.

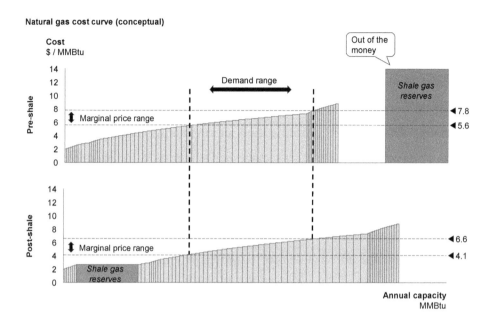

Fig. 14. The impact of shale gas on a natural gas supply curve.

The commercial exploration of shale gas, however, meant that a lot of these previously commercially unviable reserves came into the money at relatively low costs. This in turn, pushed the overall cost curve out, thus leading to an intersection point that is much lower than it was the case previously. Historically, the pricing in the United States pre- and post-horizontal drilling commercialization is shown in Figure 15 compared to Europe which has yet to complete embracing this innovation.

While the inherent volatility of the demand and supply scenarios may not have changed a lot from the past, the innovation which started around 2007 brought about a structural change in the industry and lowered overall costs and thus prices in the industry. Producers with conventional assets with cash costs of $5/MMBtu or above suddenly saw themselves being put out of the money due to an innovation in an old-world industry.

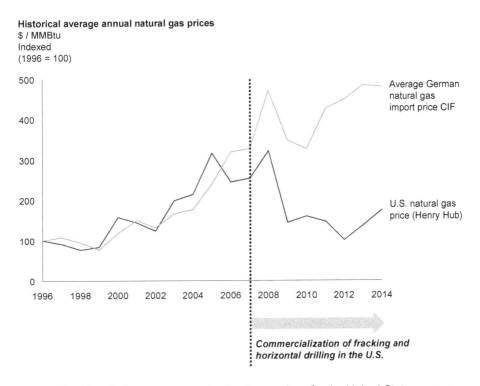

Historical average annual natural gas prices
$ / MMBtu
Indexed
(1996 = 100)

Fig. 15. The historical average annual natural gas prices for the United States versus Germany.

Similarly, the same example exists in many other industries. For example, electric-arc furnace based plants (mini-mills) versus iron ore based plants (integrated steel mills) is another classic example where using an alternate steelmaking path of making steel from scrap rendered a lot of the traditional integrated steelmakers noncompetitive who for generations have followed the path of converting iron ore and coal into steel. Out of all new steel mills that were commissioned in the United States over the last 25 years or so, only one furnace was iron ore based, which in fact was a rebuild from scratch at the site of an existing blast furnace operation.

Belief #3: All Commodities Behave Similarly

Belief #3 deals with the type of commodity itself and its use or lifetime. While the principles laid out in this book generally apply to most commodities, the one distinction that asserts itself fairly dramatically is the difference between processed and depleting commodities.

Simply put, processed commodities are those that are converted from one state to another. Some examples are steel, cement, paper, and gasoline, among others. In the case of gasoline, for instance, large refineries convert crude oil into gasoline, diesel, and other hydrocarbons by cracking and distilling complex hydrocarbon molecules into smaller ones. On the other hand, depleting commodities

# of new production sites opened, by decile

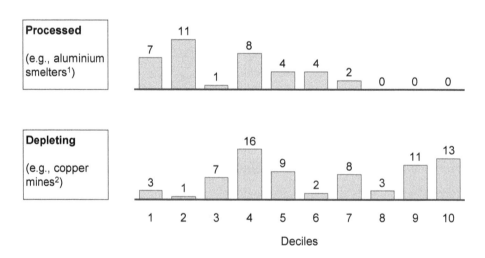

1 Deciles in even increments of capacity
2 Entry is based on weighted average of capacities added per decile

Fig. 16. New capacity additions along the cost curve for processed and depleting commodities.

are ones which have a finite asset base. The more that is being produced of a certain commodity, the less of that commodity remains. Some examples include iron ore, crude oil, copper, and nickel, among others. Depleting commodities are generally produced from mines, wells, offshore oil platforms, forests, etc.

So why are these commodities fundamentally different, even though they are both pure commodity products? It stems from the basic fact of where and how new capacity is introduced. Someone building a new steel or paper mill will always want to build a mill that is more efficient, lower cost, and more productive than what broadly exists in the market given newer technology or process improvements. Not many entrepreneurs and corporations are looking to build the next "inefficient" cement plant or petroleum refinery. Thus, most new capacity in processed commodities that enters the market is usually on the left side of the cost curve while the capacity that is being shut down is usually on the right side of the cost curve as those assets become increasingly uncompetitive and obsolete (Figure 16).

On the other hand, with depleting commodities, most new capacity is usually introduced on the right side of the cost curve. The reason is that, as natural resources are being depleted, most new production happens from deeper, further, and more complicated reserve basins, thus leading to new assets being introduced on the right side of the cost curve. Take, for example, the oil industry. In the last few years, Brazil's decision to explore and produce from the Santos offshore basin (one of the deepest offshore reserves), Saudi Arabia's decision to refine heavy crudes at its new refinery near Dammam, or the active exploration and production of oil from the Athabasca tar sands in Canada support this principle (see Figure 17).

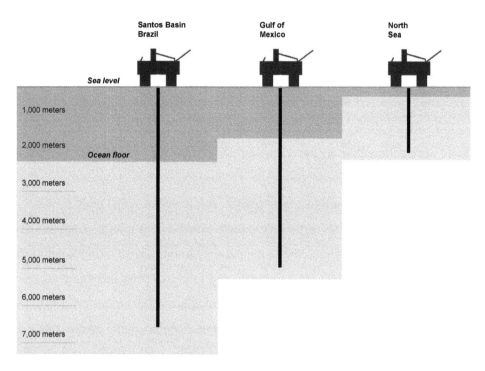

Fig. 17. Production trends in depleting commodities illustrating the increase in production cost for new assets.

This also leads us to comprehend why companies that exist in depleting commodities usually make more money than those in processed commodities. As explained above, if new assets are usually introduced on the left side of the cost curve for processed commodities, then this leads to the cost curve being flattened over time, thus reducing overall industry margins over multiple cycles. On the other hand, with depleting commodities, the cost curve will steepen over time given that new assets will generally be introduced on the right side of the cost curve. This would translate into higher returns over multiple cycles for players in these industries.

Belief #4: Inefficient Producers Who Refuse to Shut Down Don't Have an Influence On Price

Belief #4 deals with producers who refuse to shut down production capacity, even though it would make economic sense to do so. Invariably, in most commodity industries, one runs into high cost producers who are out of money but keep producing and selling at prices way below their cash cost, and yet continue to survive through these adverse conditions. Typically, these producers are state owned and/or usually do so to support large labor forces in their home countries. The cost of shutting down for some of these producers due to societal or environmental reasons far outweighs extended periods of negative profits they generate. Often, these companies cause a distortion in the cost curve methodology and they need to be treated in a way that accounts for their behavior. Consider the examples in Figure 18.

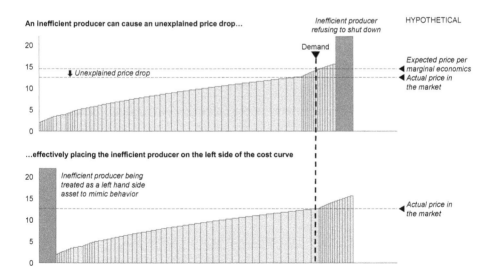

Fig. 18. Inefficient producers along the cost curve.

As shown in Figure 18, most often the producers that refuse to shut down in spite of earning negative margins over elongated periods of time need to be put at the left-most point of the cost curve. They basically represent inflexible capacity, and by treating them this way we get the cost curve to represent the industry dynamics and pricing mechanism more accurately.

To wrap up this section, one can summarize the following:

- When a high cost producer shuts down, it can often be detrimental to the industry as overall industry margins will be reduced. While the impact may be differentially felt across the remaining players in the industry, in general, it may not help the industry as it takes away from a higher pricing environment.

- The role of innovation in commodity-like industries can be game changing as witnessed in the natural gas and steelmaking industry in the last couple of decades with the introduction of horizontal drilling and mini-mills respectively.

- Over the course of a cycle, depleting commodities like iron ore or crude oil provide better returns than processed commodities like steel or cement. This is driven by the fact that newer assets get added to the right side of the cost curve for depleting commodities while they get added to the left side of the cost curve for processed commodities.

- Invariably one sees inefficient producers who defy the behavior of maximizing economic profits and who keep operating to support employment or for other reasons. Once such players are identified and their behavior is understood, the optimal way to treat them is to move them to the extreme left-hand side of the cost curve.

Now that we understand the basic tool for decoding the world of commodities (the cost curve), it is time to understand why commodity markets exhibit cyclical behaviors. The next chapter introduces the concept of cyclicality, what cycles are, and what causes them to happen.

IV. What Drives Cycles in Commodities

After introducing the concept of the cost curve and its relevance for commodity markets, we are ready to get started with one of the main concerns of commodity markets: Cyclicality, and more specifically what cycles are and what causes them to happen.

By definition, cycles refer to repeating series of events during an interval of time. In the case of economics, cycles or cyclicality usually refer to swings (ups and downs) in the price of a product or asset over time.

When thinking of a cycle, many of us intuitively think of a curve that is shaped like a sine function (see the left side in Figure 19). While this is a rather idealistic view of how cycles are shaped, it helps understand the basic elements of a cycle. As shown in Figure 19, every cycle has a certain duration (I), after which similar patterns and pricing behavior seem to emerge again. In commodity markets, a cycle is typically between 7 to 10 years long and in some cases it can be much longer. During one cycle, pricing typically shows a peak or local maximum (II) as well as a trough or local minimum (III). The difference between the peak and the trough is referred to as the amplitude of the cycle (IV). A frequently confused aspect is the difference between cyclicality and short-term volatility (V). Cycles or cyclical changes occur over several years, whereas volatility in this context refers to short-term price fluctuations that happen over weeks or months.

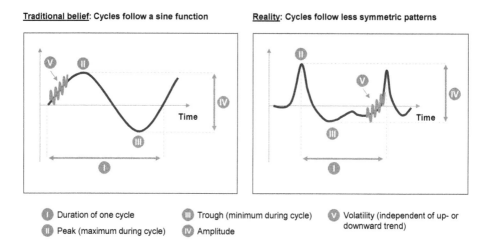

Traditional belief: Cycles follow a sine function   Reality: Cycles follow less symmetric patterns

Fig. 19. Shapes of cycles (idealistic and realistic).

While sine functions are helpful in understanding the concept of cyclicality, they have several shortcomings when it comes to understanding cycles in real markets. In reality, cycles follow less symmetric patterns and can better be described by the graph on the right side in Figure 19. Cycles are typically characterized by strong and short spikes followed by long and rather flat periods. Also, peaks typically don't have the same duration as troughs, and ascent and descent phases don't have similar but opposite slopes. This means that the shape of peaks does not mirror the shape of troughs.

The more realistic pattern of the cycle with strong spikes is supported by the following fact (see Figure 20): Considering the total margin earned by a company throughout an entire cycle of 8 years, research has shown that 50 percent of the cumulative margin is earned in only about 1 year around the peak— that is less than 13 percent of the cycle duration. The other 50 percent of the cumulative margin is earned across the remaining 7 years of the cycle. In other words, while no one can predict when it will rain in the Sahara, you better get your bucket out when it starts because this may be the only time it will rain for a

**Percent of value generated
across the cycle**
Percent

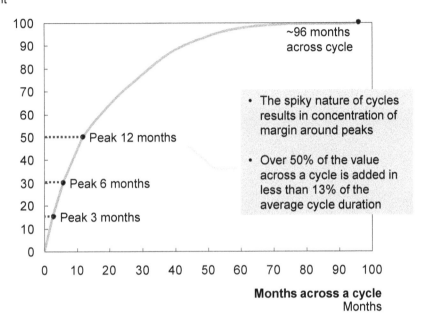

Fig. 20. Due to the spiky nature of cycles, most value creation is concentrated at the peaks.

while! Interestingly, leaders and laggards in the industry appear to show a similar profile in terms of when they accumulate their margin, even though leaders generate significantly more margin relative to laggards.

Even though the idealistic view of sine functions can lead to many misconceptions about cyclicality, sine curves are used illustratively across this book for simplicity.

After understanding how cycles are shaped and their importance to a company's through-cycle performance, let's focus on what is driving cyclicality. According to economic theory, prices are set where demand meets supply. While cyclical pricing patterns can occur in any industry, price swings are rather rare

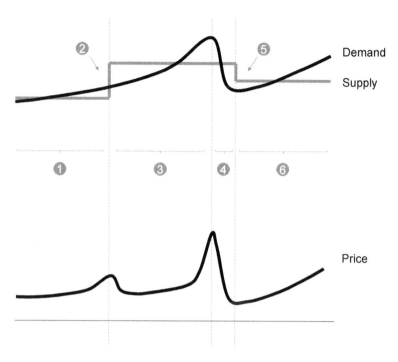

Fig. 21. Why prices in a commodity market are cyclical.

in markets where both demand and supply are consistently balanced very closely. In the case of commodity markets, however, high amplitudes of price swings are typical, which indicates frequent imbalances between demand and supply. Figure 21 illustrates supply and demand behavior in an exemplary commodity market and explains why prices are cyclical.

Any commodity-related market is likely to experience the following situations over time, exemplarily illustrated in six phases as shown in Figure 21:

1. Initially, it is assumed that demand and supply are nearly balanced. Demand is considered to be slightly lower than available supply, indicating a healthy market with no supply shortage. Now, demand is slowly starting to grow, in the case of a commodity product typically in line with

GDP. Supply remains constant because no player sees the need to introduce new capacity to the market yet. As a result, prices grow slowly but
steadily. The industry is doing well. If demand appears to be higher than
available supply, the increasing price will likely cause that either certain
customers will be priced out of the market or that products will be sub-
stituted, effectively bringing demand and supply back in balance.

2.   Once prices—and thereby margins—reach an attractive level, some
      market participant may decide to bring new production capacity online
      to sell additional volume. The new capacity can either come from ramp-
      ing up an existing site or by building a new plant. This new supply ca-
      pacity is typically not added gradually in line with demand, but in a
      chunk (lumpiness of supply-side additions). This "lumpiness" likely
      leads to the situation that supply temporarily surpasses demand.

3.   While demand continues to grow consistently, the temporary over- sup-
      ply in the market will lead to a drop in pricing. However, pricing con-
      tinues to climb thereafter, given the still strong and growing demand.
      Once demand surpasses supply again, the industry might experience a
      supply shortage, and "fly- up" pricing could incur, as previously de-
      scribed. During this typically short period of time, prices grow substan-
      tially, because consumers are fighting over the existing supply and may
      price each other out of the market.

4.   Once pricing ramps up significantly, one of two scenarios could happen.
      One possibility is that market participants introduce further capacity,
      continuing to spur the growth engine (similar to point 2). Another pos-
      sibility is that demand will drop due to extremely high pricing, poten-
      tially driven by substitutions with other, but cheaper products. A de-
      mand drop could also result from an unrelated "crisis" in the economy,

as was the case in 2008 when the financial crisis impacted the overall economy and demand for manufactured goods collapsed. While supply in a capital-intensive industry, such as a commodity, is not able to immediately follow a sharp drop in demand, the industry will face substantial over-supply.

5.   Significant over-supply almost always leads to a sharp decline in pricing. Companies typically respond by taking capacity out of the market, because they incur substantial losses from under-utilization combined with weak pricing. Production might be curtailed or entire plants might be shut down.

6.   Only when demand and supply start to re-balance, pricing will recover and become more stable. Once demand starts to pick up again relative to the existing supply capacity, pricing will start to rise again, and the industry may again be in a situation similar to point 1.

The graph at the bottom of Figure 21 shows the cyclical development of pricing as a result of a typical market behavior. As pointed out earlier, the shape of the pricing curve resembles a more realistic view about cycles than an idealistic sine function.

In this context, it is important to understand that demand and supply imbalances, and therefore cyclical prices, are only the symptoms of cyclicality. To gain a deeper understanding why cycles and cyclicality happen, we need to look at the root causes for demand and supply imbalances. The following list summarizes the factors that cause the symptoms of cyclicality:

•   **Lumpiness of changes in supply**. Bringing on new capacity or taking out existing capacity in the market oftentime result in sudden changes of large quantities given efficiencies of scale; for example, a smaller-sized steel plant in the United States has a capacity of around 2 million tons while demand grows annually at a fraction of that number. The result is always a temporary imbalance between supply and demand, causing changes in pricing.

- **Misaligned mindsets and behaviors**. Companies typically decide to add capacity when times are good ("make more money") and reduce capacity when times are bad ("save costs"). Many incentive systems of managers support this behavior. However, while this type of "herd mentality" may seem correct from a short-term perspective, it might not be the most value-adding strategy to manage through an entire cycle given that new capacity comes online or goes offline at the "wrong" point in the cycle.

- **Availability of cash**. When times are good and pricing is high, companies in cyclical markets usually utilize their money. The sudden availability of cash typically prompts further investments, simply as a means to deploy the cash. Also, many publicly listed companies face pressure from their shareholders to invest their cash and not let it sit on their balance sheets. From a through-cycle perspective, however, it might not be the best idea to add new capacity when times are good (meaning at the peak of the cycle). It may be wiser to hold on to the cash and invest it during the next trough.

- **Incorrect demand forecasts**. All strategic decisions, such as capacity additions, investments, or curtailments are driven by the company's perspective about where demand will be going. Inaccurate demand forecasts reduce the likelihood of supply and demand being in balance over time.

- **Timing of capacity additions**. Adding new capacity in a commodity market takes a long time. For example, building a new steel plant including getting all required permits can take up to 5 years or more, assuming no delays during the construction phase. Therefore, any company in a commodity market that is considering adding capacity is betting on where the market will be in 5+ years from now. The likelihood that the timing of the capacity addition is aligned with the demand cycle is very low. Capacity usually comes online too early or too late.

Many of these factors are difficult or impossible for companies to either avoid or proactively address. Some aspects that seem to favor a company's ability to successfully manage through cycles is their ability to detach themselves from "herd" behavior. This includes their ability to be independent from public capital markets. More details about which strategies work best in cyclical markets will follow in subsequent chapters.

Mining Case Study: "Lumpiness" of Supply-side Additions

To explain the concept of "lumpiness" of supply-side additions of capacity, think about a mining company. Mining companies work for years to develop new mines. On the day when a newly developed mine opens up and starts production, supply in this particular mining market will change by hundreds of thousands of tons, literally within 1 day. Typically, demand for the mined material does not increase by the same tonnage on that particular day, leading to a steep increase in supply, which could in many cases surpass demand. The new price equilibrium has shifted and a price reduction can be expected.

The reverse is true if an existing mine is closed. Supply will be reduced abruptly, whereas a corresponding change in demand is unlikely to follow at the same pace. The new price equilibrium will shift again and a price increase can be expected.

However, reality is a bit more complex. Real markets exhibit additional mechanisms that have an influence on pricing (Figure 22). Those mechanisms can either absorb extreme price swings by effectively placing price ceilings, or they can even accelerate price swings by triggering market changes.

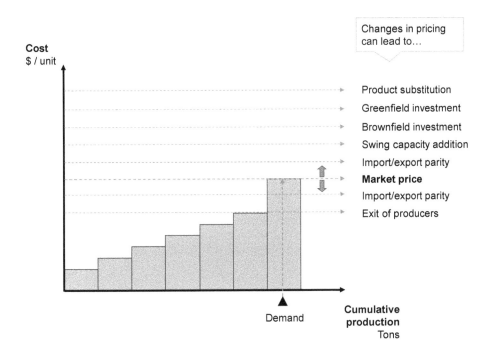

Fig. 22. The effects of price changes and respective market behavior in a commodity industry.

As shown in Figure 22, the market price usually fluctuates within a range around the cash cost of the marginal supplier. However, there are certain price ranges that could trigger additional market behavior. For example, if pricing tends to be somewhat higher or lower than the "fair" market price, import or export activity is typically stimulated. Higher prices attract imports, whereas lower prices may result in exports. If prices rise beyond import parity, market participants are typically incentivized to bring on additional capacity that can be added fairly quickly. This is called swing capacity. If prices rise further, brownfield or even greenfield investments become attractive. For even further increases in pricing, substitute products could enter the existing market to compete for revenues.

On the other side, lower prices than the "fair" market price may lead to exports—assuming demand and pricing abroad is comparable with domestic conditions—but also to the fact that producers will have to exit the market if prices do not allow for sustainable margins.

At this point, let's take a pause. We have learned a lot about the economic fundamentals that drive pricing and cyclicality. With all this knowledge, the question arises: Can pricing—and therefore cycles—be predicted? After extensive research around cyclical pricing behavior and a wealth of available knowledge and tools to analyze cycles and pricing, our conclusion is that it is not possible to accurately predict pricing on a consistent basis.

For example, we have compared the accuracy of market price predictions for several commodities, including zinc and aluminum. We compared the forward prices of these commodities at various points in the future with the actual prices at that time in the future. We realized that over the short-term, pricing can be estimated fairly correctly, with correlations between forward and actual prices being as high as 80 or 90 percent for 3-month forward pricing. However, for forward prices beyond a 3-month forecast period, the accuracy to predict the market rapidly declines. Adding 12 months, the correlation between forward and actual prices declined to nearly 50 percent. Adding another 24 months reduced the accuracy to 10 percent or less. This means that forward curves can serve as a good indicator of a "point in time" market sentiment.

However, forward curves should not be used as a leading indicator for price predictions for the future. For instance, research in the nickel market has shown that forward curves over time have consistently been in backwardation, indicating a consensus of declining prices, whereas the nickel spot price has actually turned out to show significant volatility with substantial ups and downs over time.

Case Study: Can You Predict Natural Gas Prices?

Ever since the beginning of the shale gas revolution, the price of 1 MMBtu of natural gas at the Henry Hub has typically fluctuated between $3 and $5, with $4 being a reasonable average. Consider the following case:

A company that consumes a lot of natural gas, such as an integrated steel producer, can spend up to $70 million/year on natural gas for an average-sized manufacturing facility. Assuming the price for natural gas is currently at $4/MMBtu, what would you advise this company to do? Should they lock in their entire consumption at a fixed price for $4, thereby protecting the company from being hit with possibly $5 natural gas or even higher prices? Or should they buy their entire consumption in the spot market, hoping to benefit when prices drop to $3/MMBtu or less?

One real-world example that we have observed was a company that decided in 1 year to adopt the first strategy, that of locking in their entire consumption when prices were right below $4/MMBtu. This was at the beginning of 2012 when the United States experienced a very mild winter, leading to prices for natural gas dropping to less than $2/MMBtu. Needless to say, the company was locked in at $4 when the market price was $2, leading to a lost opportunity of nearly $15 million for the company. The following year, the same company adopted the exact opposite approach. When gas prices recovered to $4/MMBtu during the subsequent winter, the company decided to float 100 percent with the market, believing that prices could drop again to $2. Due to weather-related demand in early 2013, prices for natural gas were rising temporarily closer to $5/MMBtu. The company again lost a couple of millions of dollars.

The takeaway: Even large corporations are oftentimes incapable of accurately predicting commodity prices. Even if they get it right once, they typically do not have a consistent track record of being right. Very often, we have observed corporations taking a position on commodity prices that turns out to be different than originally anticipated. It would be wiser to accept the fact that you cannot predict the cycle!

To conclude this chapter, let's recap some highlights:

- Cycles are often mistaken as sine functions. In reality, however, cycles show different patterns with strong spikes and long, flat periods. Most of the value generated throughout the entire cycle is made in a very short period of time.

- Cycles are driven by five primary factors: Lumpiness of changes in supply, misaligned mindsets and behaviors (herd mentality), availability of cash, incorrect demand forecasts, and the timing of capacity additions. In reality, pricing is driven by many other mechanisms, including imports and exports, swing capacities, brownfield and greenfield investments, substitute products, or producers exiting the market.

- Cycles cannot be predicted. Attempts at doing so might only reasonably work over the very short term, but any price prediction for more than 1 year is likely to be inaccurate. Also, track records of consistently accurate price predictions are uncommon.

In the next chapter, we will use the material presented so far to debunk some commonly held beliefs around what would be good strategies in commodity markets.

V. Top Ten Insights About Companies Beating the Cycle

After understanding the concept of cost curves and why cycles happen, we will now introduce some insights on how successful companies are able to create value in cyclical commodity markets. Based on research and our own first-hand experience in the industry, we have concluded that many successful players are successful because they have broken with traditional and intuitive concepts of how to operate in cyclical commodity markets. We have summarized a Top Ten list of counter-intuitive insights that have proven to be most effective. The Top Ten insights on how successful companies are able to beat the cycle are:

(1) **Sit out the cycle**. The value of selling a production asset and not operating it may be higher than operating it through a downcycle.

(2) **Build a war chest**. Holding onto cash reserves through a cycle allows for deploying capital at the right moment when other sources of financing might be difficult to access.

(3) **Buying is better than building**. Independent of the timing of the cycle, buying assets is generally superior to building them.

(4) **Get on the "commercially efficient frontier."** Depending on the company's desired level of risk, value creation can be optimized across raw materials and sales contract portfolios.

(5) **Go private**. Many barriers to successful through cycle management are caused by incentive systems of public equity markets.

(6) **Avoid consensus-based decision making**. Averaging opinions ensures mediocre results. Limit final decision making to a small group.

(7) **Optimize your footprint**. Building an empire is not necessarily the same as generating value in commodity markets.

(8) **Stop obsessing about operations**. While bad or inefficient operations represent a tremendous downside risk for the company, the upside opportunity from other cycle strategy levers is much greater.

(9) **Diversify your management team**. Diversity is a powerful tool for creating high-performing companies; however, commodity industries are far behind others.

(10) **Don't over-estimate the power of vertical integration**. Be selective when integrating vertically. It is not always the cure-it-all medicine it is made out to be. In fact, it often destroys value if done for the wrong reasons.

Sit Out the Cycle

Cyclicality usually refers to fluctuations of the sales price of a commodity product. However, not only does the price of the commodity fluctuate, but also the price of the production asset itself, as well as the price of the underlying company's stock.

Figure 23 shows this relationship for gasoline and refineries for the last full cycle in oil and gas. As the graph illustrates, the amplitude of cyclical volatility of the production asset (refineries) in terms of asset value is higher than the amplitude of the price of the commodity product (gasoline). Taking this insight one step further, it effectively means that there might be arbitrage opportunities between the value of the production asset and the commodity price. For instance,

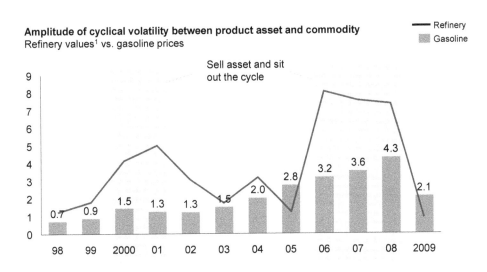

Amplitude of cyclical volatility between product asset and commodity
Refinery values[1] vs. gasoline prices

1 Equivalent to the implied value per daily barrel of acquired refining crude processing capacity

Fig. 23. Refinery values versus gasoline prices.

Source: J.S. Herold, Platts, Natural Gas Week, team analysis.

the value of selling the production assets may be higher at certain times during the cycle than the value of keeping and operating the asset through a downcycle. Subsequently, a strategy focused on selling assets could offer significant opportunities for value creation.

However, to capture this arbitrage opportunity, companies need to be prepared to sell their production asset instead of operating it for the remainder of the cycle. While this strategy of sitting out the cycle might create significant value, it requires guts and good foresight. The strategy is counter-intuitive, given that the asset would need to be sold during a time when the market is doing well and the asset is likely generating healthy margins. Executives rarely have an incentive to sell well-running cash cows.

The higher volatility of upstream assets compared to downstream commodity prices also allows for significant value creation not only from selling but also from buying assets. If implemented consistently, this can effectively translate into an asset-trading strategy.

An example of an industry where the decision to trade assets is crucial is freight airlines. Freight airlines constantly need to evaluate the value of the assets in their industry (airplanes) relative to the market prices of the commodity service offered (freight rates). Similar to refineries and gasoline, the value of an airplane typically fluctuates much more than freight rates. This might also lead to the opportunity to create significantly more value by buying and selling airplanes compared to maintaining a traditional freight business throughout the cycle. Some freight airlines have been constantly exploring the opportunity of asset trading for years, constantly making trade-off decisions between buying or selling airplanes versus owning or leasing them, all depending on where current freight rates are in the cycle.

While the upside potential from trading assets can be significant, the risks associated with it are equally as high. Selling or buying an asset at the wrong point of time in the cycle can turn out to be a very costly mistake. Also, an asset trading strategy entails that a company believes it can predict the future of the cycle which contradicts the other main insights of this book. Pulling this off needs companies that adopt the mindset of an asset trader when thinking of their entire asset base. This means that while many commodity companies traditionally view themselves as manufacturers of commodity products, these companies consider themselves as a company that holds a set of assets that create or destroy value relative to the position in the cycle with the associated downside risks. Such good companies have the managerial courage to let go of assets when the time is right which we refer to as timers in a later chapter about winning archetypes for navigating through cycles.

In summary, sitting out the cycle and selling assets at or near a peak in the cycle sounds counter-intuitive but could provide for significant value. A few points should be considered as takeaways:

- Not only the price of the commodity product itself, but also the value of the asset that produces the commodity product fluctuates. The amplitude of value increases the more upstream you go. Therefore, selling an asset at a certain point in the cycle might create more value than operating the asset through the next downcycle, effectively allowing for an arbitrage opportunity. The reverse logic is true for buying an asset.

- Astute forecasting abilities to time the sale (or purchase) of an asset are necessary. If asset values are not correlated with the commodity product or service price, additional insight would be required to track both markets. An efficient decision-making process is critical to capture the optimal value between peak and trough.

- While the upside of trading assets is high, the risk associated with an asset-trading strategy is also high. Therefore, a successful asset-trading strategy rather deals with adopting the mindset of an asset trader than with the actual trading of assets; good companies adopting this approach have the courage to sell assets at the right time.

Build a War Chest

As we learned in the previous chapter, an effective asset-trading strategy requires a company not only to sell assets, but also to buy assets at certain points during the cycle. Obviously, a company should buy an asset at or near the bottom of the cycle. One caveat of this strategy is, however, that the company would need to come up with significant capital during a time when margins are low or even negative, and capital markets may consider the industry to be unattractive. Even though the opportunity might exist to buy a "cheap" asset, cyclical commodity markets entail the risk that capital might not be available to finance such a transaction at or near the bottom of the cycle. For example, the steel industry faced an extremely dire situation between 2009 and early 2013, with many companies losing over 90 percent of their market capitalization and possibly even facing bankruptcy. Capital market participants had limited faith in the industry and investments in steel almost completely dried up for years, even though many assets would have been available at relatively low prices.

One way to address the issue described above is by holding onto excess cash on the balance sheet. Particularly in commodity markets, however, any excess cash is typically rare and therefore in high demand when it becomes available. The opportunity cost of not deploying the cash is wrongfully considered to be high. Publicly listed commodity companies especially feel pressure from their shareholders to deploy excess cash by either investing it or paying out dividends. Holding onto cash reserves seems like a counter-intuitive strategy to many executives and shareholders.

Figure 24 shows the liquidity level of companies that have been successful throughout the last cycle in their respective industries. Liquidity level is defined as the ratio of cash and short-term investments over total assets, and it should give an indication to what extent those companies are holding onto their cash. The successful players ExxonMobil, Methanex, and Vedanta all show above-average liquidity levels, indicating that they preserve a higher portion of their cash compared to average players in their industry. Anecdotal evidence also suggests that private companies, such as Koch Industries or Cargill, pursue a rather conservative cash-management approach and hold onto significant excess cash

Liquidity level[1]

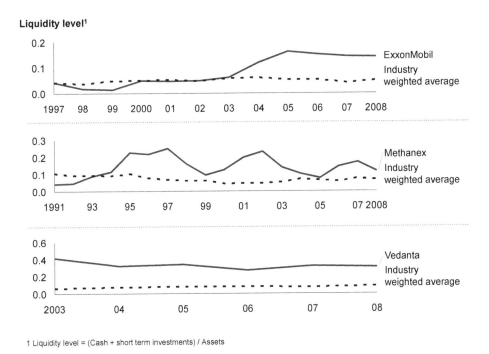

1 Liquidity level = (Cash + short term investments) / Assets

Fig. 24. Successful companies are characterized by having higher-than-average liquidity levels.

reserves because they don't feel the pressure to deploy the capital at wrong times in the cycle.

Another reason for building and holding onto a sufficiently sized war chest includes the opportunity to benefit from arbitrage opportunities between the commodity market and capital market. For instance, debt markets typically do not exhibit a close correlation with pricing in commodity markets. In other words, the cost of debt is typically not related to the product price in a commodity market. This means that companies can borrow when cheap debt is available—independently of where they are in the commodity cycle—and then hold onto the cash to invest it when commodity prices are low. Understanding both the credit spread cycle and the commodity cycle at the same time helps companies better identify the optimal time period to finance future investments.

In summary, there is a strong incentive for companies in cyclical markets to develop and maintain significant cash reserves that may be deployed at the right time in the cycle. The takeaway of this section can be summarized as follows:

- An effective asset-trading strategy includes not only selling but also buying assets, ideally at or near the bottom of the cycle. This requires the availability of capital during times when margins are low and capital markets might consider the industry to be unattractive.

- Holding on to excess cash provides for a counter-intuitive, yet successful strategy to be able to pick up "cheap" assets when times are rough and availability of funding might be tight. For successful companies to preserve a higher portion of their excess cash, they must resist the pressure from public equity markets to deploy their cash at sub-optimal times.

- Debt markets and commodity prices typically do not show a close correlation, and therefore they allow for arbitrage opportunities. Companies can borrow when debt is cheap, independent of where they are in the commodity cycle. The cash raised can subsequently sit on the balance sheet and can be deployed when commodity prices are low.

Buying is Better Than Building

When investing into an asset, companies have many options how to go about it. In addition to debottlenecking or increasing throughput at an existing production site, they can invest into new capacity by either buying an already existing facility or building a new one. This situation refers to the well-known dilemma of "buy versus build." While the right answer for buy versus build is typically not straightforward, the answer in commodity markets is much simpler: Buying assets is generally superior to building them.

The rationale for this statement is based on the following logic. A company can make the decision to buy or build a new asset at any time during the cycle. For simple reasons, we looked at three random points in the cycle:

- **Top of the cycle**—"typical" behavior caused by cash availability and herd mentality.
- **Any time throughout the cycle**—"average" behavior when market participants don't know if pricing will go up or down.
- **Bottom of the cycle**—"optimal" behavior, but rarely observed in practice.

For all three scenarios, we have used simulation analysis to compare the internal rate of return of a typical buy versus build project (Figure 25). The simulation was based on the following assumptions: the investment needed for buying and building the asset is the same; building the asset would take 3 years; and the timing of building the project is uncertain as well as the pricing in the market at the time when the asset comes online.

The analysis revealed: The build strategy is at best on par with the buy strategy at the top of the cycle ("typical" scenario); however, the buy strategy outperforms the build strategy in all other scenarios. The reasons are multifold, with the three most relevant reasons being the following:

- Building new capacity adds new supply to the market. Based on the insights from previous sections, new capacity in the cost curve leads to an overall price reduction in the market which needs to be taken into account when comparing the financial attractiveness of both buy and build options. This price reduction would not happen when an existing capacity is bought. In contrast to building, buying only leads to a change in ownership of the asset, not a change in the available capacity in the market.

- Building a new asset takes significantly longer than buying an asset. For example, building a new plant can take at least 3 to 5 years if not significantly longer, whereas the acquisition of an existing plant can

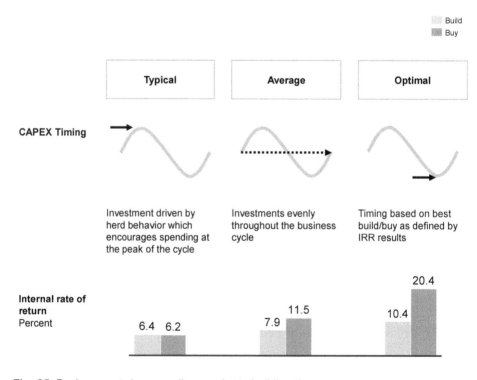

Fig. 25. Buying assets is generally superior to building them.

be done in just a few months. Due to the longer time and uncertainty to bring new capacity online, the company's ability to correctly predict the demand cycle at the time when the new capacity comes online is significantly reduced. The faster execution of buying an asset allows for compensating for a lack in forecasting accuracy. Based on simulation analyses, the increased uncertainty about the timing of the capacity addition leads to a significant discount of the value of the asset from a through cycle perspective.

- Building new capacity entails a significant risk for cost overruns. Especially for capital-intensive commodity markets with thin margins, cost overruns by a few percent can be very harmful for the overall project net present value (NPV). When buying an asset, however, the purchase price for the asset is known at the time of the decision making. It is adjusted only for changes in working capital or other liability issues which are typically marginal. For a new build, cost overruns are common with wide variations in terms of their magnitude. In other words: When buying, you know what you pay, when building, you don't know what you will end up paying. Taking this uncertainty of cost overruns into account significantly worsens the build scenario.

The primary downside of buying an existing asset compared to building it includes the age of the equipment and therefore its remaining lifetime as well as its adaptability to technological change. In commodity markets, however, manufacturing equipment typically lasts for long periods of time. For example, many of today's steel plants were built 100+ years ago. Also, significant changes in technology do not occur as frequently. Having said that, in case of an industry-wide technology leap, building a new asset could be beneficial over buying an existing asset. The cost of the new equipment will typically be lower than the cost to retro-fit an existing asset and to bring it up to par with the new standards. One example is the threat that steel producers face as auto companies are substituting steel with more light-weight materials, such as aluminum. In order to compete and avoid the substitution of steel, steel companies are forced to develop new, light-weight steels, so-called advanced high-strength steels (AHSS), or ultra high-strength steels (UHHS). These steels can typically only be produced with new equipment that allows, for example, for the continuous annealing of the steel itself, a process that makes the steel thinner but harder and therefore stronger with less weight. Investments in new production lines are typically required.

In summary, in cyclical commodity markets, buying an existing asset is generally superior to building a new asset. Key points to consider are:

- Building is only comparable with buying at the peak of the cycle, when the premium paid for an existing asset likely over-compensates for the downside risks of building.

- In all other cases, buying is superior to building in commodity markets for three main reasons: (i) no new capacity is added which is beneficial for pricing; (ii) timing of execution is faster, reducing the likelihood of incorrectly predicting the demand cycle; and (iii) risk of cost over-runs is lower, given that the final price is known at the time of the deal.

- Building only allows for benefits over buying in case of a technology leap that can only be addressed with new equipment.

Get On the "Commercially Efficient Frontier"

Another insight as to why some commodity companies are more successful than others has to do with how they manage their commercial exposure. Commercial exposure typically refers to contracting approaches in procurement and sales. Together, they represent a significant driver of financial performance of a commodity company, with 60 to 80 percent of total cost of sales typically being related to raw material purchases.

In an ideal world, companies purchase raw materials at the lowest price and sell their finished products at the maximum price possible. From a contracting perspective, companies have a multitude of options to actively manage their commercial exposure, including spot pricing, fixed pricing, indexed pricing, cost plus pricing, and many other options. For simplicity, this chapter will focus only on the two most relevant options to buy raw materials or to sell finished products: Spot price and fixed price contracts.

Depending on where you are in the cycle, it might be obvious what the best contracting strategy is (Figure 26). From a sales perspective, if you are at the top of the cycle (A) you want to be exposed 100 percent to spot pricing in the market to be able to fully capture the benefit of high prices in the industry. By contrast, at the bottom of the cycle (B) you would prefer to have no exposure to spot pricing; any price that was locked in previously at a higher level will pay off at that time. The answer is similar, yet reversed, from a procurement standpoint.

Obviously, those answers can only be given after the fact. In reality, however, the situation is more complicated. Companies constantly find themselves in position (C), where it is not clear if pricing will rise, remain constant, or decline. The optimal portfolio is unknown at this stage.

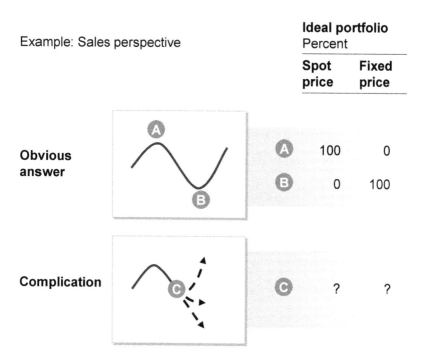

Fig. 26. Ideal contracting portfolios based on position in the cycle.

When a company is at point (C) in Figure 26, it can pick any combination of spot and fixed price contracts for both procurement and sales. The question arises what is the optimal contractual exposure at this point in the cycle?

To get started, let's focus only on the procurement side. We will add the sales side later on. Figure 27 shows a simplified and exemplary overview of the different options available to structure pricing of procurement contracts. For example, a company can choose to be exposed with 10 percent of their purchased volume to spot prices and for the remaining 90 percent to have fixed price contracts in place (equivalent to strategy P-2). Even more extreme, the company can increase their spot market exposure to 100 percent of their total purchasing volume with no fixed price contracts in place (strategy P-11).

Procurement contracting portfolio		
	Spot price Percent	Fixed price Percent
P-1	0	100
P-2	10	90
P-3	20	80
P-4	30	70
P-5	40	60
P-6	50	50
P-7	60	40
P-8	70	30
P-9	80	20
P-10	90	10
P-11	100	0

Fig. 27. Combinations of possible procurement contracting strategies (percent of volume).

In that context, it is critical to take a step back and highlight one important aspect: Every time a company decides to fix pricing, to float with the spot market, or to take any combination thereof, the company is taking a position on their perspective where prices will go in the future. The company is effectively taking a "bet" on the future price developments. For example, consider a company that purchases large quantities of zinc, and current zinc pricing is at $1/pound. If this company decides to buy 100 percent of next year's zinc requirements on the spot market, this company is effectively taking a "bet" that the price of zinc will be at or below $1/pound for the next year (inflation-adjusted price). The reverse is true if the company would lock in 100 percent of their zinc requirements at a price of $1/pound. This means that the company is taking a "bet" that the inflation-adjusted price of zinc will be above $1/pound in the next year.

This way of thinking about taking positions in the market is shedding a different light on the definition of risk when hedging prices. Conventional thinking assumes that locking in prices is considered to be equivalent with reducing risk, because you already know today what your future price will be. However, the example above illustrates that locking in prices does not necessarily reduce risk; just imagine the company is locked in with 100 percent of its zinc volume at $1/pound and the price of zinc drops below $1/pound for the entire next year. The result will be hurtful, even though the company had the certainty of knowing that their price will be exactly $1/pound for the entire year. Therefore, locking in prices only reduces uncertainty, but not necessarily risk.

Going back to our example in Figure 26, the question was: What is the optimal portfolio mix of spot and fixed price contracts? The answer to this question is neither obvious nor trivial, given that each portfolio of spot/fixed price contracts entails a different risk profile. To find an answer for the optimal contracting portfolio, it is helpful to apply tools from portfolio theory. One of the most well-known concepts in portfolio theory is the "efficient frontier" model. For portfolios with different risk profiles, the efficient frontier approach helps identify the portfolio that offers the highest expected return for a given level of risk, or vice versa, the lowest level of risk for a given return. Using simulation analysis, the risk/return profile of each contract portfolio can be determined.

In the following paragraphs, we will describe a simulation analysis that evaluates all portfolios P-1 through P-11 listed in Figure 27. The simulation analysis was done in a real-world corporate context for buying natural gas. For simplicity reasons, the analysis focuses on optimizing the purchasing decision for 1 month into the future, based on the available forward pricing in the market at the time of the analysis. The results of the simulation analysis delivered a perspective on the risks and returns of each portfolio P-1 to P-11. Return is thereby defined as

Return (Mean)
Percent

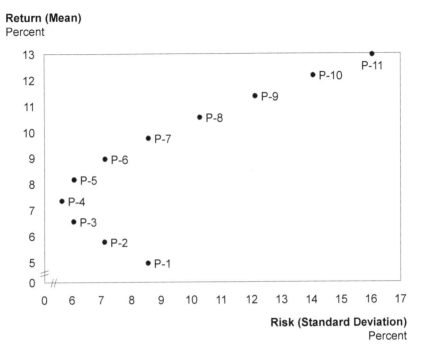

Risk (Standard Deviation)
Percent

Fig. 28. Exemplary risk/return profiles of different spot/fixed price portfolios for buying natural gas (time horizon: 1 month into the future).

the incremental value generated by fixing X percent of the natural gas volume for the following month at today's forward prices compared to the decision of not fixing any pricing. Risk describes the standard deviation of the return. The result of the simulation analysis is shown in Figure 28. The results reveal the following insights:

- Portfolios P-1 through P-11 all have different risk/return profiles based on the then-current forward prices for natural gas in the market.
- Portfolio P-11 (100 percent spot, 0 percent fixed pricing) exhibits the highest relative return, but also the highest risk.

- Portfolio P-1 (0 percent spot, 100 percent fixed prices) exhibits the lowest return, but not necessarily the lowest risk. For the same level of risk, portfolio P-7 offers a significantly higher return. This leads to the conclusion that portfolio P-7 has a superior profile to P-1.

- Portfolio P-4 offers the lowest risk, but it still shows a higher return than portfolios P-1, P-2, and P-3.

- While portfolio P-11 offers a higher return than portfolio P-4, the associated risk is nearly two times higher than the expected return. The same is true—to a lesser extent—for portfolios P-6 through P-10, when compared with portfolio P-4. Only portfolio P-5 seems to have a comparable risk/return profile to P-4 (higher return, but also a proportionately higher risk).

This leads to the conclusion that any rational manager should either pick portfolios P-4 or P-5 when deciding how to structure the mix of spot and fixed price agreements for natural gas for the upcoming month based on a risk/reward perspective. This means that between 60 to 70 percent of the natural gas volume should be bought at fixed prices. The remaining 30 to 40 percent should float with the market.

The same analysis can be repeated for any month in the future to determine a month-by-month hedging strategy for the next 12 months or more. Remembering the rapid decay in the accuracy of forward pricing, it is usually not advisable to focus on evaluating optimal portfolios for much more than 1 year into the future. Of course, current market conditions need to be considered, such as forward pricing being in contango or backwardation, as well as additional costs, such as financing costs of forward contracts or storage costs in the case of fixing prices for physical goods.

Similar to the analysis for procuring natural gas, a company's sales contracting approach can be optimized using an efficient frontier model to determine the optimal portfolio from a risk/reward perspective. Many companies, however, are hedging out price risk from procurement and sales activities individually and separately. In an extreme scenario, this could lead to situations where a company is fully hedged with 100 percent fixed price contracts on the procurement side, but 100 percent exposed to spot market conditions on the sales side. Small corrections in the market, such as a simultaneous reduction in raw material prices and sales prices, can have a significantly negative impact on the company's profitability through the cycle. Therefore, a well-rounded contracting strategy should always take both ends of the spectrum into account simultaneously when hedging contracting risks, procurement contracts and sales contracts.

Of course, the complexity to identify optimal procurement and sales portfolios simultaneously increases exponentially. This is where the real fun starts! The following framework, however, can help identify an appropriate strategy and visualize common pitfalls that should be avoided. First, let's look at the different options available for a company to structure their procurement and sales contracts (Figure 29). As in the previous table, the company can chose different portfolios on the procurement side (P-1 through P-11). Similarly, it can also structure different contracting portfolios on the sales side (S-1 through S-11).

With the exemplary contracting strategies P-1 to P-11 and S-1 to S-11 in mind, let's try to answer the question: What is the optimal mix of spot and fixed price contracts for both procurement and sales contracts simultaneously? Instead of optimizing for the individual answers for each, Figure 30 shows how the different permutations of procurement and sales contracting portfolios interact with each other.

	Sales contracting portfolio	
	Spot price Percent	Fixed price Percent
S-1	0	100
S-2	10	90
S-3	20	80
S-4	30	70
S-5	40	60
S-6	50	50
S-7	60	40
S-8	70	30
S-9	80	20
S-10	90	10
S-11	100	0

	Procurement contracting portfolio	
	Spot price Percent	Fixed price Percent
P-1	0	100
P-2	10	90
P-3	20	80
P-4	30	70
P-5	40	60
P-6	50	50
P-7	60	40
P-8	70	30
P-9	80	20
P-10	90	10
P-11	100	0

Fig. 29. Combinations of possible contracting strategies (percent of volume).

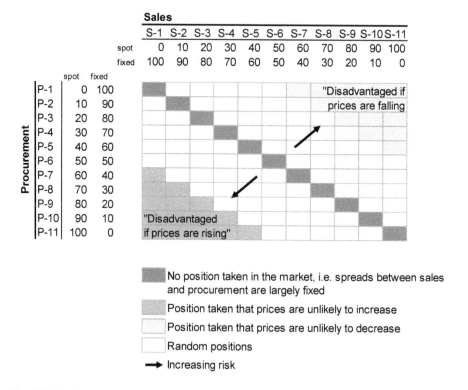

Fig. 30. Positions for different spot/fixed price contracts for procurement and sales.

Figure 30 looks very complex and needs some explanation. The procurement strategies P-1 through P-11 are shown on the left axis, whereas the sales strategies S-1 through S-11 are shown on the top axis. As a result, all exemplary permutations of the procurement and sales contracting strategies together are shown in the center. The main conclusion that can be drawn from Figure 30 is the following: While taking a position in either procurement or sales individually can be described as being equivalent to "betting" on where prices are going, the combination of procurement and sales contracting strategies can allow for a natural hedge against that "bet" by eliminating the risk of taking a position.

The reason is as follows: Assuming prices for raw materials and finished products are somewhat correlated, which they typically are to a certain extent in commodity industries, selecting the same contracting strategy for both procurement and sales allows for effectively fixing the spread between the sales price and the raw material price. To explain this in more detail, think about a company that chooses to fix prices for 80 percent of their volume for both raw material purchases and sales of finished products. For this 80 percent, the spread between the sales price and the raw material price is effectively locked in, because the prices for both are already known and will not change. The remaining 20 percent of the raw material cost and sales are exposed to the spot market. Assuming sales prices and raw material prices are correlated and move up and down in sync, the spread between the raw material price and sales price is effectively fixed as well, independent of where market prices are going. This means that as long as the procurement contracting exposure and the sales contracting exposure follow the same ratio of spot versus fixed pricing, the company has a natural hedge against cyclical pricing by effectively locking in the spread between sales price and raw material price. This strategy is considered to be the lowest risk strategy, because the company is not taking any position in the market. The combinations for the same procurement and sales contracting strategies are illustrated in Figure 30 by the dark grey area (diagonal line).

If the procurement and sales contracting exposure differs, the company is effectively moving away from the diagonal, "low risk" line, and starts to actively take a position in the market. This increases the company's risk profile. The highest risk profiles exist for contracting combinations with opposing ratios for spot/fixed price contracts, which means either 100 percent fixed sales prices with 0 percent fixed raw material prices, or 100 percent spot sales prices with 100 percent of raw material cost locked in at fixed prices. Those extreme scenarios are illustrated in Figure 30 by the light grey areas in the corners of the chart. If a company finds itself in a position where all of their sales contracts are locked in at fixed prices, but all their raw material costs are floating in the spot market, the company has effectively taken the position that the industry is headed to the bottom of the cycle. By contrast, if a company finds itself in a position where all of their sales contracts are spot contracts, but at the same time all the raw material costs are locked in, the company has taken the position that it is headed to the top of the cycle.

To conclude this logic, the further a company moves away from the diagonal, "low risk" line, the larger the "bet" that the company is making and the higher the company's commercial risk profile. While any combination of fixed/spot price contracting along procurement and sales is practically doable, companies should be aware of the risk/return profiles that they are subsequently taking. Taking into account the logic of the efficient frontier model, higher returns usually come at higher risks, and the optimal portfolio is usually close by the lowest risk portfolio (see Figure 28 above). In order to optimize the risk/return balance, the takeaway for a company is therefore to align the procurement and sales contracting exposure respectively. As a concrete example, if your sales portfolio

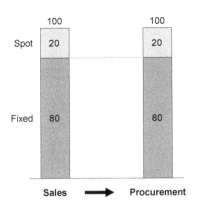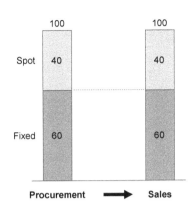

Fig. 31. Optimization of risk/return profiles across both procurement and sales contracting exposure (percent of spot versus fixed price contracting exposure).

consists of 80 percent fixed price contracts and you would like to minimize your risk exposure, you should attempt to lock in 80 percent of your raw materials at fixed prices. Alternatively, if your raw material contracts call for 60 percent fixed price agreements with the remaining materials being purchased at spot pricing, you should aim for a sales portfolio that is 60 percent fixed and 40 percent spot pricing if you want to minimize risks (see Figure 31).

To optimize a company's commercial contracting exposure, one final question remains: When should I have a high(er) exposure to spot prices and when a higher exposure to fixed prices? The respective asset's position on the cost curve gives an answer. Keeping in mind the shape of cycles and the fact that commodity companies make the vast majority of their through cycle margin during peak times, a low-cost asset should be more exposed to spot than fixed pricing for the following reason: They can capture the full, over-proportionate upside of upswings while they only under-proportionately hurt during bad times. By contrast, the more you move towards the right side of the cost curve, the incremental value from capturing margin during good times declines, whereas the risk of being

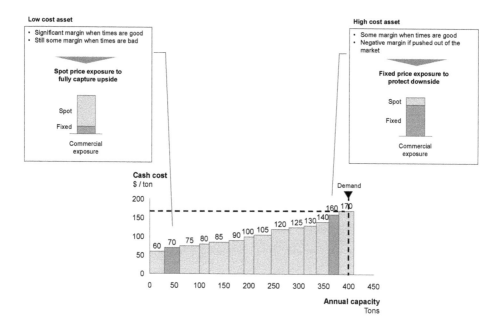

Fig. 32. Desirable exposure to spot/fixed contracting depending on the asset's position on the cost curve.

pushed out of the market increases. The risk of being pushed out of the market becomes over-proportionately higher than the upside from being exposed to up-swings in the cycle. It might therefore make sense to lock in a certain spread across procurement and sales to be safe from the risk of being pushed out of the money. This means that the fixed portion of the procurement and sales contracting exposure should increase for assets that are more on the right-hand side of the cost curve (see Figure 32).

This chapter has been long and provides a lot of complicated information about finding the optimal commercial contracting exposure. However, it is probably also one of the most critical chapters in terms of understanding a new, perhaps counter-intuitive way of thinking about cyclicality and the desired level of exposure to risks and cyclicality.

In summary, the main takeaways of this section are:

- Commercial contracting exposure in procurement and sales is a significant driver of the financial performance of a commodity company. Companies have a multitude of options to actively manage their commercial exposure, including spot pricing, fixed pricing, and many other options.

- By deciding on a certain contracting approach, a company is always taking a position in the market and is effectively "betting" on future price developments. Locking in prices is oftentimes confused with reducing risk. However, it only reduces uncertainty, but not necessarily risk.

- In order to find the optimal spot/fixed price combination for either procurement or sales contracts, an efficient frontier simulation analysis can help identify the optimal portfolio based on the desired risk/return appetite. Efficient frontier analysis has been successfully applied in financial portfolios for many years; however, multi-billion dollar commodity companies seem to rarely utilize this tool to optimize their contracting portfolios, even though the insights can be equally valuable.

- Complexity increases if procurement and sales contracting are optimized together. The combination of both procurement and sales contracting, however, allows for one significant advantage, namely for a natural hedge against "betting" on future price developments. Assuming prices for raw materials and finished products are somewhat correlated, the same contracting approach for procurement and sales allows for eliminating the risk of taking a position in the market. Any move away from the lowest risk contracting combination increases the company's commercial risk exposure.

- The optimal exposure to spot versus fixed price contracting depends on the asset's position on the cost curve. In general, lower cost assets should enjoy more spot price exposure to fully capture upside, while higher cost assets are safer with a higher portion of fixed price contracts.

Go Private

One of the questions we have pursued for years includes the question about what is the appropriate corporate and capital structure to be successful in a cyclical market. Many people intuitively think that publicly traded companies are better equipped to deal with cyclical markets due to their typically larger size combined with the more rigorous financial discipline which is imposed on them by capital market participants. While size is definitely an important factor in determining a company's success in cyclical markets, we have come to the conclusion that publicly listed companies usually face many barriers to implementing a successful strategy that maximizes shareholder value through an entire cycle.

The three most common barriers that prevent public companies from being able to successfully manage through cycles are:

- **Misalignment of reporting cycle and commodity cycle**. Cycles in commodity markets can last 7 to 10 years, sometimes even longer. A successful through cycle strategy may require that some decisions are taken with a long-term investment horizon in mind to maximize value through the cycle. Public companies, however, report earnings every

3 months. The entire company's performance—and therefore executives' compensation—is evaluated based on those quarterly or annual earnings. This makes it very difficult to provide appropriate incentives to managers to pursue projects that could generate higher NPVs based on a 7- to 10-year through cycle time horizon, but which do not necessarily generate the highest returns for the next quarter. Management is therefore compelled to ignore longer-term investments in favor of shorter-term wins. Companies might be forced to adopt suboptimal decisions from a through cycle perspective.

- **Inability or unwillingness to stockpile capital**. When times are good is when commodity companies generate most of their excess cash throughout the cycle. Being a publicly traded company, shareholders usually get concerned when too much cash is sitting on a company's balance sheet and they may request a payout of excess cash in the form of dividends or stock buybacks. While this could benefit the company's stock price over the short term, this approach is myopic when looking at the next downturn, which will come inevitably. During the next downturn, companies need excess cash not only to survive the downturn, but also to have enough firepower to invest when prices are low and additional assets could be picked up at lower valuations. From a through cycle perspective, the optimal decisions to handle excess cash might be counter-intuitive to most shareholders' appetite for cash distributions.

- **Herd behavior for investments**. During a peak in the cycle, companies' profits look attractive and valuations of publicly listed companies typically increase significantly. To maintain a high share price, companies typically think about further growth at this stage, partly because pricing looks attractive and no one wants to think about the next downturn when times are good. During these periods, shareholders and managers frequently believe that new investments should be made. In return, however, this means that investment decisions are typically made based on cash availability, and not when great opportunities arise. Even worse, adding capacity at the peak of the cycle typically leads to a skewed investment proposition, by limiting further upside but at the same time under-stating the possible downside risk. In addition, the nature of herd-based investing at the top of the cycle often drives up asset prices. Especially in public equity markets, it is difficult to convince shareholders that investments should be made when times are rough.

Considering these barriers for the implementation of a successful through cycle strategy could help explain the success of privately held companies, such as Cargill, Glencore (pre-IPO), or Koch Industries.

Privately held businesses are able to pursue their investment strategies independent of pressure for conforming behavior from public equity markets. Those companies are able to buy assets and businesses at times when no public shareholder would be interested in investing, because they can pursue longer-term investment horizons. Moreover, this gives them the ability to pick up "cheap" assets, because competitive pricing for assets and businesses is minimal during downturns in the cycles they operate in.

In summary, the following conclusions can be drawn about the right corporate and capital structure for a successful through cycle management strategy:

- While the size of a company is definitely important to provide for stamina to navigate through an entire cycle, a public listing on stock markets does not seem to set the right incentives for a successful through cycle strategy.

- The most common barriers faced by public companies to manage through cyclical commodity markets include: (i) Misalignment of the reporting cycle with the commodity cycle, (ii) the inability or unwillingness to stockpile capital, or (iii) herd behavior for investments leading to investing at the wrong time in the cycle.

- Those barriers to successful cycle management should be consciously addressed to avoid detrimental effects. Therefore, privately held companies might have a natural advantage over public companies when managing through cyclical commodity markets.

Avoid Consensus-based Decision Making

One critical and often overlooked aspect in cyclical commodity markets is execution of the company's strategy. Conventional thinking believes that commodity markets have a longer term horizon and changes do not happen very quickly. While most of this is true, it wrongfully implies that speed in execution might not be a characteristic of a successful commodity company.

Counter-intuitively to this common belief, timing of execution is actually very crucial in cyclical markets. The longer the execution of a strategic project takes, the further is the delivery of the expected results from it. This significantly reduces the likelihood that predictions for demand and supply at the time when the project comes online are accurate. For example, if a company plans to build a new plant, it makes a big difference if its realization takes 2 years or 5. Predictions of demand and supply for 5 years into the future are significantly more inaccurate compared to predictions for a 2-year time horizon. Most financial models underlying the investment decision are likely to be incorrect. Therefore, fast execution not only enables companies to better time the cycle but also to compensate for a lack in forecasting accuracy.

Real-world examples have shown that successful commodity companies continuously outperform their peers in terms of timing of the execution of large investment projects. For instance, ExxonMobil is known for developing new oil fields faster than their peers, with the Sakhalin 1 field taking only 30 months, whereas its competitors needed 75 months to develop Sakhalin 2. Another successful company known for its speed in execution of investment projects is Vale. Between the mid-1990s and mid-2000s, Vale built a total of seven power plants, all of them within a 2 to 3 year time frame. The average build times for power plants can easily be twice as long. In addition, Vale brought the Sossego copper mine online in June 2004. The $1 billion project was completed in only 24 months, 3 months ahead of schedule.

The question now arises how companies can ensure a timely execution? When asking this question, we have come across another counter-intuitive insight. While many large companies base their decision making on consensus-based approaches involving many functional or regional areas within a company, successful commodity companies often take the opposite approach: Decision-making of cycle strategy and strategic projects is done in small circles. For example, the following quote was made by an equity analyst covering ArcelorMittal:

> "To go from one steel plant in Indonesia to buying the biggest steel company in the world could only have been pulled off by Lakshmi Mittal. Operating in public equity markets or organizational democracies often can take the wind out of one's sails..."

At ExxonMobil, almost all major capital decisions are made by one core team. Vedanta's decision-making process is known to be very efficient and fast given that major capital decisions are usually limited to three to five people. Vedanta has a clear demarcation between capital and commercial decisions that are made at the top level in the company versus operational decisions that are made at the business unit level.

Another privately held company, however, has a unique model that has proven to be successful; it follows a very entrepreneurial approach combined with streamlined decision making at the corporate level. Discovery and origination of opportunities happen in a dispersed group of entrepreneurs and businesses across the entire corporate universe. This so-called "spontaneous order" generates many different points of view that will be shared across all their businesses through peer review challenges. The company's flat organizational structure helps offset the typical bureaucracy and time delays associated with this type of decision making. Overall, this sharing of best practices among a broad base of entrepreneurs within and across the organization has helped the company find the optimal path for value creation across all its businesses.

In summary, most through cycle winners limit the cerebral portion of their through cycle strategy formulation and execution to a core group of people. Averaging opinions across many participants, especially in large corporations, ensures mediocre results, even though idea generation and discovery should happen in a broader context. In more detail, the takeaways of this section are as follows:

- Against common belief, speed in execution of large investment projects is crucial in commodity markets. Being late in the cycle can often cost billions of dollars.

- One of the main benefits of speed in project execution allows companies to compensate for a lack in forecasting accuracy of future demand and supply cycles.

- Successful companies limit decision making for strategic projects to a core group of people. While idea generation can happen among a broad base of employees, successful companies don't appear to rely on consensus-based decision making when it comes to cycle strategy formulation and the execution of their large strategic projects.

Optimize Your Footprint

Every company, not just companies in commodity markets, is constantly facing the question of how to increase profitability and shareholder value. In almost every case, senior leadership follows the common belief that "growth = value creation." This vision holds true in many industries; however, it can be harmful in commodity industries. In other words: Building an empire is not necessarily the same as generating value. The following example will explain this counter-intuitive insight in more detail (see Figure 33).

The exemplary industry is structured as follows: Seven plants (A through G) exist in the market. They all produce the same commodity product. The total industry capacity is currently at a little over 400 tons, and demand is at around 370 tons/year. This makes plant G the marginal producer in the market. Looking back at the explanations about cost curves, the market price is set by the marginal producer, which means by the cash cost of plant G which is $220/ton. Therefore, all plants in this market are able to sell their products at $220/ton.

Our exemplary company AB Steel now owns plants C and F. Plant C produces 70 tons/year with cash costs of $85/ton, and plant F produces 50 tons/year with

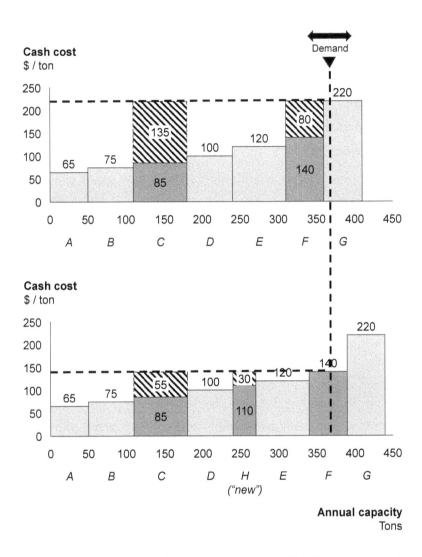

Fig. 33. The possible impact of "building an empire" on profitability in a commodity market.

cash costs of $140/ton. With the market price being at $220/ ton, AB Steel makes a profit of $135/ton with plant *C* and $80/ton with plant *F*. This translates into a total profit of $13,450/year for the company.

Now, the CEO of AB Steel wants to increase his profitability. To do so, he follows the "growth = value creation" paradigm, and he plans to expand his capacity by building a new plant. Shortly thereafter, AB Steel brings the new plant *H* to the market, which is located somewhere in the middle of the cost curve. Plant *H* brings another 30 tons of capacity to the market, taking AB Steel's overall capacity from 120 tons to 150 tons, which increases its footprint by 25 percent. The intuitive belief is that this move will increase AB Steel's profitability, as long as the plant is positive from an EBITDA/ton perspective. However, let's have a closer look at what the real result of this move will be:

- Introducing plant *H* will move plant *G* out of the market, making plant *F* the new marginal producer.
- The cash cost of plant *F* is now setting the price in the market. This means the market price will drop from $220/ton to $140/ton.
- This reduces the profit per ton for AB Steel's plants to $55/ton for plant C, $30/ton for plant *H*, and $0/ton for plant *F*.
- As a result, while AB Steel's total capacity increased by 25 percent, its profits fall by nearly 65 percent to only $4750/year.
- On top of that, AB Steel would need to use a portion of their profits to cover the capital cost for the new plant *H*.

The example shows that increasing your footprint and "building an empire" can actually destroy value. Hence, empire building is very different from value generation in commodity markets. This might be counter-intuitive to the ego of many executives. In some cases, a smaller footprint may actually increase profitability even though it could reduce the CEO's domain.

In summary, when thinking about the optimal size of a company in a commodity market, corporate leaders should keep the following in mind:

- "Growth = value creation" does not always hold true in commodity markets.

- Simple price-setting mechanisms in commodity markets can lead to the fact that new capacity does not add value for the producer, but it can over-proportionately shift value downstream to the customer by reducing overall pricing in the market.

- Finding the right size that maximizes absolute profitability can even mean reducing your company's footprint.

Stop Obsessing About Operations

Traditionally, the management of a commodity company cares about three things: Operations, Operations, and Operations; more particularly, reductions in fixed and variable operating costs or some tactical price changes to adapt to market shifts. Historically for many companies, the almost exclusive focus on operations has many reasons. One of them is that operations represents the company's core process of turning raw materials into finished products. Therefore, operations plays a major role in terms of people resources. Up to 90 percent or more of all employees in a commodity company can have a role in the company's operations, directly or indirectly reporting to the management of a plant or production site. In return, this also means that current and prospective candidates for management positions across the company are very likely to be recruited from a previous operations role, simply because operations represents the largest pool of a company's talent. While there is a lot to be said about management's knowledge and experience about the company's core processes, the following question needs to be addressed: Out of all functions to run a business, what are the most critical ones to maximize value for the entire company?

Research that we did revealed yet another counter-intuitive insight for many operators. Using extensive simulation analysis for companies across different commodity industries, we have analyzed what the most important functional levers are to add value to a business in a cyclical commodity market. The answer was surprising: The impact of improvements in operational performance was comparatively small. While operations is certainly an important factor for any commodity company, the inherent upside potential from other functional levers was considered to be much greater. For instance, buying and selling assets at the right time in the cycle has proven to provide by far the largest impact on a company's valuation. Also, a company's approach to commercial contracting is a much more relevant lever in terms of value creation than operations. Other strategic levers that were more crucial for improving a company's value than operations included the company's capital strategy (including decisions about cash reserves, dividend policies, and debt leverage) as well as the company's capacity management strategy (de-bottlenecking or curtailing).

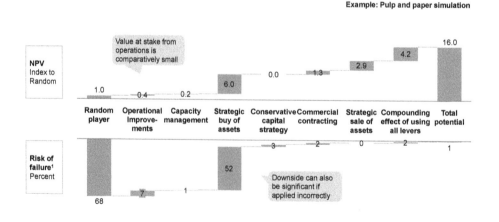

Fig. 34. While operations is important, the value at stake from other cycle strategy levers is much greater.

Figure 34 exhibits the results of the simulation for an exemplary pulp and paper company. The chart shows the simulated NPV of a random company in the pulp and paper industry relative to the company's risk of failure as defined by the company's likelihood to run out of cash during the full cycle of the simulation. The first simulation was run for a random strategy (random player), that means no cycle management lever has been actively pulled. The result is shown at the left-hand side of the chart: Its NPV has been indexed to 1, and the risk of failure was about 68 percent, which means that in 68 percent of all simulations, a random player would have run out of cash at some point during the full cycle of the simulation. Subsequently, we have "switched on" certain levers that were considered to have an impact on the company's performance throughout the cycle. The impact of each additional lever can be seen by following the chart towards the right. The incremental benefit of the resulting NPVs of the simulation for each additional lever was indexed to the NPV of the random strategy. The results show: Switching on additional cycle management levers consistently increased the company's NPV while it simultaneously reduced the company's risk of failure. Using all levers at the same time (compounding the effect of all levers) nearly increased the value creation potential by a factor of 4×. Overall, using all cycle management levers allowed the exemplary company to increase its NPV by a factor of 16× while it reduced the risk of failure from 68 percent to around 1 percent. As pointed out above, the results illustrate the humbling influence of operations (operational improvements) compared to the other cycle strategy levers.

We were surprised about the results of the simulation analysis as well, especially having worked ourselves in industrial environments for many years where operations is always considered the "silver bullet" of a company. When looking for reasons why the upside potential from operations was comparatively small, one explanation could be that operational improvements have been the focus at many companies for decades already. The incremental improvements by squeezing out another cent in the cost of sales per ton is rather minimal. By contrast, other levers have systematically been neglected for decades, such as improving the company's commercial exposure along procurement or sales contract portfolios.

Certainly, while the other levers, such as buying and selling assets, have shown to provide for significantly more upside than operations, they also entail significant risk. Buying an asset or selling an asset at the wrong time in the cycle can destroy tremendous value. However, when thinking about a risk/return perspective, the risks and returns seem evenly distributed for mostly all levers; with one exception: Operations. While operations provides for very limited upside potential, it entails a tremendous downside risk. One cardinal mistake in operating plant equipment could cause an entire plant to shut down, and in the worst case, can make an entire company go out of business.

In summary, the takeaways of this section are:

- Traditionally, commodity companies heavily focus on improving operational performance. While operations represents a crucial functional area in any commodity company, leadership should ask themselves if operations is the functional area that can deliver the most incremental value to the business.
- Research has shown that other functional levers have a much more significant importance for creating value, such as buying and selling assets, commercial contracting, capital strategy, or capacity management.

- Even worse, besides the limited incremental upside potential coming from operational improvements, operations provides for a tremendous downside risk. While operations represents the ticket to the game for any commodity company, a simple failure in equipment can have a devastating impact on an entire company, effectively making operations a company's biggest wild card.

Diversify Your Management Team

The insights of the previous section can be taken even a step further. While the previous section revealed that an almost exclusive focus on one functional discipline (operations) might not necessarily unlock a company's full value potential, the same is true for any type of diversity, for example, age, gender, or ethnicity.

For instance, it is a widely known fact that diverse leadership teams perform better than non-diverse teams. A recent McKinsey study has found that companies with a high proportion of women in leadership roles perform significantly better than companies with no women in leadership positions. The results were stunning: Companies with top-quartile representation of women in executive committees generate on average 47 percent more return on equity and on average 55 percent more earnings before interest and taxes (EBIT).

A closer look at diversity at commodity companies reveals alarming insights. A 2014 report by Forbes Magazine shows that traditional commodity industries, such as basic materials, utilities, industrials, and oil and gas rank lowest in terms of representation of women in boardrooms of S&P 500 companies (see Figure 35).

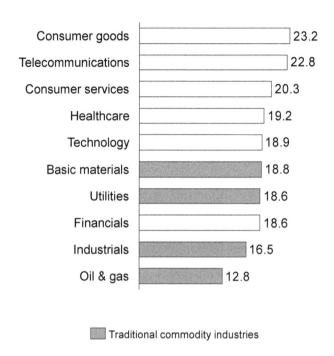

Fig. 35. Women inside the S&P 500 boardrooms (percentage of female board members).
Source: Forbes Media, Gender Map, 2014.

According to Forbes, the oil and gas industry faces the worst gender diversity issue with an overall average of only 5.7 percent female board members. None of the oil and gas companies on the S&P 500 have more than 25 percent female board members. Four companies, such as Chesapeake Energy and Diamond Offshore Drilling, have no women on the board at all. In conclusion, changes are urgently needed in these industries, not just in the entire workforce, but also on the highest decision-making levels.

While this insight might not be very surprising, it is surprising, however, that no company in a commodity industry has actively addressed this issue yet. In their defense, many companies in these fields face problems hiring a diverse workforce, given the low representation of women in technical majors in schools and universities. Even the boards of companies like Google and Facebook do not show an ideal gender diversity. However, those technology companies are actively working on improving their diversity, knowing about the potential to unlock value from diverse teams. Prominent examples include Marissa Mayer (CEO, Yahoo!), Meg Whitman (CEO, HP), Virginia Romett (Chairman and CEO, IBM), or Sheryl Sandberg (COO, Facebook).

In this context, diversity isn't restricted to gender diversity alone. Age, race, sexual orientation, as well as ethnic diversity have proven to be significant drivers of companies' performances. It is up to the commodity companies to follow the lead of their technology counterparts as well as other companies, if they aspire to unlock the power of diversity.

In summary, the insights of this section are as follows:

- Diversity—in particular diversity in senior leadership positions— has proven to be a powerful driver in a company's performance.
- Commodity industries, however, are lagging far behind other industries in terms of diversity. While most technology- and engineering-related companies are facing challenges when hiring a diverse workforce, other high-tech companies in similar situations are leading the way in transforming their workforce.
- If commodity companies are serious about trying to unlock the full potential of value creation, a significant shift in the composition of their boardrooms has to happen.

Don't Over-Estimate the Power of Vertical Integration

We almost made it through this chapter! While we have by now learned about how successful—and counter-intuitive—approaches to navigating cycles look like, one topic is still missing. It deals with the concept of vertical integration.

CEOs of commodity companies can get very frustrated with highly volatile prices for either their raw materials or finished products. As we have learned, unexpected swings of certain prices can have a substantially negative impact on a company's performance—and therefore executives' compensation— even though the company might be operating flawlessly. This risk is oftentimes conceived as a negative phenomenon, and many CEOs try to mitigate that risk. Besides locking in pricing—as we have discussed previously—another solution would be to vertically integrate into raw material or finished product markets. This would immediately take out exposure to price volatility, and earnings become much more predictable. Examples of vertical integration in commodity markets are fairly common with most vertical integrations happening upstream into raw materials. Examples include steel companies buying mining assets, oil and gas producers investing in oilfields, or paper companies investing in forests to access pulp and wood.

While vertical integration allows making earnings more predictable, it does not necessarily optimize a company's financial performance from a risk/return perspective. Parallels can be drawn to the commercial strategy where we talked about locking in prices via fixed price contracts; commercially speaking, vertical integration is similar to buying fixed price contracts, with the exception that the company is not entering into a contractual relationship but an ownership relationship with the supplier or customer. Therefore, vertical integration fundamentally differs from a purely contractual exposure to vertical markets, and vertical integration should typically be done only because of any of the following four reasons:

- **Possibility of vertical market failure**. A company should vertically integrate if it faces the situation that either its raw material or finished product markets are exposed to vertical market failure. This means the company has no choice in securing an alternative contract at arm's length with its suppliers or customers which results in the company's inability to negotiate a contract under a fair pricing mechanism. An example would be a company owning a mine that is served by only one rail line with no other economical solution to transporting the mined material out of the mine. Negotiations between the mining company and the rail line operator are not characterized by fair pricing mechanisms and neither the mining company nor the rail line operator would be able to secure a contract at arm's length at fair market conditions. A vertical integration of the mining company into the rail business or vice versa can help avoid the possibility of vertical market failure.

- **Security of supply or demand**. Even if raw material or finished product markets operate under fair pricing mechanisms, there is another reason why companies might want to consider vertical integration. For instance, when raw material or finished product volumes in the market are not sufficient to allow the company to conduct its core business, vertical integration might make sense. One example would be when the European power industry was contemplating large-scale investments into biomass-fired power generation, based mainly on the use of wood pellets. Given significant subsidies for biomass power in Europe, many European utilities were planning to build significant generation capacity from biomass-fired power plants. The expected increase in generation capacity far exceeded the economically sustainable available resources for wood in Europe. Even though there was an existing and functioning market for wood pellets in Europe, the available supply for wood pellets was nearly 10 times less than the newly anticipated demand in the market. As a result, many European utilities had no choice but to vertically integrate into forestry assets (via investments or other forms of concessions) as well as equipment, such as pelletizing capacity, because a lack of available volume would have resulted in a lack of pricing. In extreme scenarios like these where markets face insufficient volumes, there won't be a price that will clear the market. It should be kept in mind, however, that unexpected changes in subsidies could significantly worsen the economics of this vertical integration, and proceeding with caution might be appropriate.

- **Influence on value chain**. Besides avoiding vertical market failure or securing supply and demand, another reason why a company should vertically integrate deals with additional benefits from the integration that allow for influencing the economics of the company's core business. For example, the company ChemCo is a large producer of chemX (disguised for confidentiality reasons). However, the company's real differentiation in the market comes from its extensive logistics network—in particular, ChemCo owns and operates the largest fleet of tankers for chemX in the world (at some point they had 19 tankers). This substantially increased the company's effective capacity in the market by allowing ChemCo to accommodate a large portion of demand volatility by relatively small modulations of their production and logistics capacity. Without the footprint in the specialized logistics network, the opportunity to modulate capacity would be significantly smaller, and ChemCo's ability to manage capacity at the right times in the cycle to grow demand for their product would be much more limited. Therefore, vertical integration makes sense if the additional benefits from modulating capacity through adjacent parts of the value chain outweigh the cost associated with achieving the vertical integration.

- **Synergies**. Last but not least, the more obvious answer why vertical integration makes sense has to do with synergies. The combination of two entities in the same industry— either upstream or downstream from each other—can create economic value as long as the incremental margin from one business outweighs the additional cost of capital of the other business; in simple terms: if $1 + 1 = 3$, a company should vertically integrate. However, the estimation and realization of synergies oftentimes leads to failure of vertical integration by an ineffective deployment of capital. The following paragraphs will explain this rationale in more detail.

Of the four reasons for vertical integration mentioned above, most managers vertically integrate because they believe in their ability to realize synergies. However, in many cases the synergies from a vertical integration don't materialize. In fact, what many vertical integrations fail to consider are dis-synergies, meaning the ineffective deployment of capital. Let's consider the following case example in Figure 36. The graph compares a time period of 14 years (from 1993 to 2007) of the total return to shareholders (TRS), the return on invested capital

(ROIC), as well as the EBIT margin of four different players in the pulp and paper business: (i) upstream-related businesses (forest and pulp assets), (ii) pure play paper companies, (iii) integrated paper companies, and (iv) downstream-related businesses (end users of paper products). The results reveal the following: Pure play paper companies show the worst performance, whereas upstream- and downstream-related businesses show the best performance. Integrated players show a slightly better performance than pure play paper companies, but still a significantly worse performance than upstream- or downstream-related businesses. This means if you are an investor in a pure play paper company, do you want your company to vertically integrate? The answer would obviously be "No" as long as you have the chance to invest separately into the upstream or downstream business yourself and capture the significantly higher returns. The numbers point towards an inefficient use of shareholders' capital when companies integrate vertically. While the performance of being an integrated company looks better than being a pure play company, the shareholders would have lost out significantly in terms of deploying their capital in the most attractive option.

In addition to the ineffective way of deploying capital, the true performance of the individual businesses gets diluted, mainly by intransparent transfer pricing between subsidiaries of an integrated company. This means that shareholders face the risk of investing indirectly into a bad performing upstream business that looks like a good paper business, or vice versa, investing indirectly into a bad paper business that only looks like a good performing paper business because it gets subsidized by co-owned upstream assets. In short, each business needs to perform well on a stand-alone basis, and true synergies can only be captured if the integrated company is able to offer some value to customers that they would otherwise not be able to get on the market—and subsequently pay for. This is very difficult to achieve in commodity markets.

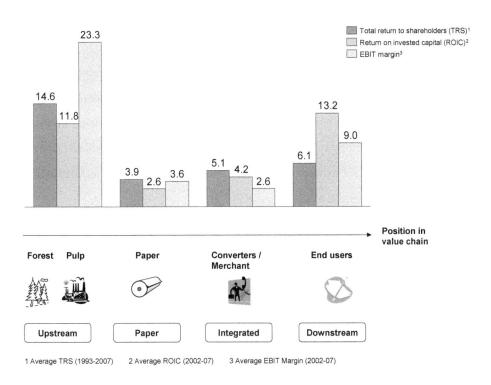

Fig. 36. Vertical integration could imply an ineffective use of capital.

In summary, we have learned the following in this section:

- Vertical integration represents an opportunity to reduce exposure to the cyclical pricing of raw materials or finished products. However, similar to locking in prices via fixed price contracts, vertical integration reduces uncertainty but comes at a risk.
- Only under a few circumstances, vertical integration might make sense. Those circumstances include: (i) the possibility of vertical market failure, (ii) the security of supply or demand, (iii) the influence on the value chain, or (iv) synergies.

- Frequently, the value of synergies is over-estimated leading to ineffective deployment of capital. Transfer prices not aligned with market prices will lead to nontransparent reporting of an integrated company's performance; one business might therefore subsidize the performance of another business, giving the market an inaccurate picture of the company's overall performance. From a shareholders' perspective, each business of an integrated company should perform well on a stand-alone basis.

Until now, we have learned about the power of cost curves in commodity markets, why cycles happen, and how successful companies in cyclical commodity markets behave. In the next chapter, it's time to put everything together and see if we are able to make good judgments ourselves if we were to find ourselves in the shoes of an executive or the CEO of a commodity company.

VI. Putting It All Together: Applying What We Learned

Now that we understand how commodity markets behave and the different elements of value creation, let's put them all together to test our hypotheses. To get started, let's first revisit the example that we used before and refer to the exhibit in Figure 37.

For a brief moment, let's assume that you are the CEO of the manufacturer Circle, and you own two production plants A and B on the extreme left side of

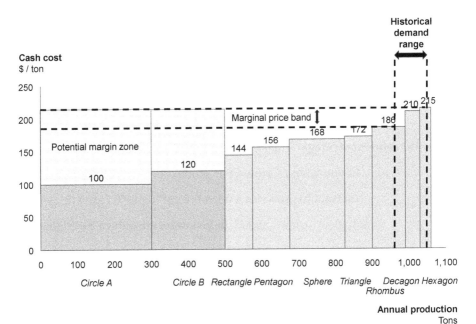

Fig. 37. An exemplary industry environment for a commodity company.

the cost curve. Obviously, you have one of the healthiest positions in the industry as a starting point with your plants having demonstrated the ability to earn between $66 and $115/ton annually, given a historical marginal price range between $186/ton and $215/ton. Now, it is your task to set up the direction and the vision of the company for the next 8 years to the board, investors, and your employees.

Let's break down the different decisions you will make into a shorter list:

1. **Commercial strategy**: What commercial exposure would you like the organization to aim for on both procurement and sales? How much spot and fixed price business would you like to take on both ends? This can then be translated and made more granular by your teams into which segments to serve, or what offerings to put together.

2. **Capital strategy**: Given that you sit at the head of a company that generates a lot of cash from operations, the questions facing you are:

   a) How much cash do you want to give back every year to investors? What's the dividend/share buyback policy?

   b) How much debt do you want to take on your books?

3. **Investment strategy**: The two critical questions facing you here are:

   a) Do you want to grow your production footprint or reduce it? If you want to grow, then do you want to pursue growth by acquisition or a new build? If you want to reduce your footprint, which asset do you want to sell or shut down?

   b) Do you want to spend money on innovation, and if yes, how much?

4. **Operational strategy**: Obviously, the question that you have to grapple with here is split across three dimensions:

a) How do you plan on splitting your resources and production time between preventative maintenance and active production?

b) If you had a choice of selling two types of blends (a richer blend and a normal blend), what is the right mix of blend you want to sell?

c) How do you plan on compensating your employees— cyclically adjusted (after all why should they be penalized for a bad year of pricing) or cyclically unadjusted (they make more when years are good and vice versa)?

5. **Talent and organizational strategy**: Finally, who should be part of your team and why? Will the majority of your team consist of your most experienced operators who know the operations and manufacturing really well or someone else? And if it is someone else, where and how will you find and retain this talent?

As you have probably gathered by now, these are not easy questions to answer and this list is definitely not exhaustive. The list above is probably a small subset of the most important questions that someone looking to manage a commodity- or asset-intensive industry needs to answer.

As you are making up your mind on the questions above, let's share the decisions that we have seen top management teams make to the questions above and understand the consequences of the same. After that, we will provide a case study of the turnaround of the fourth largest flat steel company in the United States, Severstal North America. One of us was given the opportunity to be the CEO of that company where we actively implemented several of the strategies and levers presented so far.

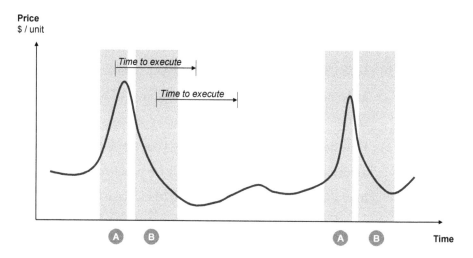

Fig. 38. Exemplary points during a cycle for making critical decisions.

To first describe the decisions that most top management teams are making, consider the two most exciting parts of a cycle (see Figure 38): A— when prices are rising and rising fast, and B—when prices are falling and falling fast. Usually, most critical decisions are made during these periods which change the overall trajectory of the company for the remainder of the cycle.

Let's assess just three snippets of the typical decisions management teams make during the period A when prices are rising:

- **Commercial strategy**: Management decides that they want to unwind their existing fixed price sales contracts and maximize exposure to the cycle by selling on the spot market. However, in reality, the organization takes time to unwind these contracts and data shows us that by the time these decisions are implemented, the peak has passed with the market now moving to period B—the one of falling prices. So, effectively, while the decision may have been right at the time, by the time organizations get around to implementing it, they get full exposure to the spot market near the bottom of the cycle.

- **Capital strategy**: Top management teams and CFOs actually seem to feel pressure when times are good and earnings are rising to show uses for the cash being generated. They are often pressured to come up with growth or investment options, or else the governing logic usually states that the cash has to be returned in the form of dividends, stock buybacks, or other means. Doing this often leads the company to reduce its cash on hand, inhibiting its ability to stockpile capital for the lean years, thus being unable to make good acquisitions when the cycle bottoms out.

- **Investment strategy**: Our observations of most players in commodity markets reveal that most players decide on adding or buying new capacity in an era when prices are rising. This is also the time when assets, whether being built or being bought, are most expensive. Unfortunately, especially for the ones building new assets, these assets get commissioned when the cycle has already peaked and is probably closer to the bottom, thus making the original investment thesis fairly weak.

Similarly, let's assess the same three decisions during period B when prices are falling:

- **Commercial strategy**: Management decides that they want to minimize the volatility of their earnings and try to manage downside risk. It's at this time that they go back to their long-term customers and offer them longer-term fixed-price contracts with a slight premium to the current spot prices in the market. On the buy side, this is a time when they try and renegotiate with their vendors to reduce costs of their fixed-price contracts to more accurately reflect the spot market. In summary however, this often leads to locking in longer-term fixed-price contracts on the sales side and greater exposure to the spot market on the buy side. The key to doing this well and successfully, however, is determined by the time taken to fully execute these decisions from the time a decision is made, which is typically where most organizations lose value.

- **Capital strategy**: These moments are especially scary for management teams, and most go into the mode of capital conservation and cost cutting. They start saving cash and cut out important but often considered discretionary spending areas like reliability-centered maintenance. Some public companies also find themselves forced to pay dividends in spite of dire balance sheets as they feel not doing so would adversely impact their share prices. Some may even be forced to sell their assets to stay alive, especially if their commercial contracts do not provide for any relief compared to market pricing.

- **Investment strategy**: This is usually the time that most players are not looking to invest in new capacity as they go into cash-conservation mode. Unfortunately, a lot of them are actually forced to sell some of their better assets at low prices just to stay afloat and pay bills.

As you can see above, firms demonstrate fairly different decisions and behaviors at different points in the cycle. As you apply these decisions in Circle's case, one can statistically prove and understand why there is a high probability that one of the most healthiest players in the industry could cease to exist in a matter of a couple of cycles. One of the critical insights that was derived from the simulation model that was developed for the paper industry—as presented earlier—indicated that the probability of failure over a 16-year period of a player that made random decisions as shown above was as high as 68 percent. Extrapolating this to the case above, most of the decisions taken in this example actually may raise the probability of failure above 68 percent given that they are executed poorly.

That leads to the key question of what can firms and management teams do in this scenario. Consider the following decisions which remain unchanged through the cycle—meaning they remain constant in an environment of rising and falling prices and everything in between.

- **Commercial strategy**: Management decides that given the low cost position of their assets, they want to remain fully exposed to the cycle. This translates into the company striving for a 100 percent spot book on the sales side giving the organization the maximum volatility in terms of earnings. While this may seem counter-intuitive even when prices are falling, this company will generate the highest margins across the cycle compared to its competition in most scenarios. A corresponding procurement strategy needs to be adopted as well to optimize the risk exposure for the entire commercial contract portfolio.

- **Capital strategy**: Management decides that they would like to stockpile capital on their balance sheet instead of being forced to make suboptimal investment decisions (especially when prices are rising) or give it back to shareholders to adhere to a dividend policy that may not make sense. This decision coupled with the decision to remain fully exposed on the commercial side ensures that this organization would enter the bottom of the cycle with one of the strongest balance sheets in the industry.

- **Investment strategy**: The management implements a disciplined investment strategy which centers around the philosophy that they will only make acquisitions when the assets being bought make a return relative to the long-term equilibrium price of the commodity they produce. For example, consider that the cycle is on the upswing and the asset being considered is priced at $500 million while the current price of the commodity it produces is $100/unit. However, the organization's long-term equilibrium price for the commodity is $60/ unit. While the investment may make sense with a price consideration of $100/unit, it doesn't make any sense when prices are $60/unit. At this point, the company decides to pass. Similarly, on the flip side when markets are falling and the price of an available asset is $200 million and the commodity price is $40/unit, the company decides to acquire this asset as their long-term pricing is $60/unit. The implication of this philosophy is that over time, someone with the respective cash reserves will pile up a set of low cost-efficient assets over multiple cycles.

To put the insights above into a real-world context, let's look next at the turnaround story of the steel company Severstal North America during 2013 and 2014.

Case Study: The Turnaround Story of Severstal North America

A CEO'S PERSPECTIVE

Severstal North America (SNA) was the United States subsidiary of the Russian metals and mining giant OAO Severstal. OAO Severstal employed some 70,000 people worldwide with $15 billion in revenues, having a major footprint in mining (iron ore and coal) as well as flat rolled steel.

SNA represented approximately $4 billion in revenues, 2500 employees, and nearly 6 million tons of flat rolled steel production capacity. The company operated two steel plants, one integrated steel mill in Dearborn, Michigan, and one electric-arc furnace steel mill in Columbus, Mississippi. In September 2014, SNA was successfully sold for $2.3 billion to AK Steel and Steel Dynamics.

One year prior to the sale, the authors of this book had been put in place as part of a new management team that included the position of the CEO as well as several key VP positions. Within 12 months of taking the lead in managing the business, free cash flow had been turned from a negative number into a positive net cash flow of nearly $150 million on an annualized basis. Also, total EBTIDA grew by over 100 percent while only 20 to 30 percent of the increase was explainable by changes in market pricing.

But let's start at the beginning. When the new management team took over in the late summer of 2013, steel pricing in the industry was close to a 5-year low, nearly at price levels directly following the 2008 economic crisis (see Figure 39).

The starting position was anything but promising. However, I had taken a few bold steps right at the beginning, followed by a consistent implementation of several additional measures. Referring back to the Top 10 counter-intuitive insights presented earlier, I had actively addressed nearly all levers during my first few months as CEO. The only levers that I had not been able to address were asset trading, buying/building of new assets, or vertical integration because of strategic considerations and timing in the cycle.

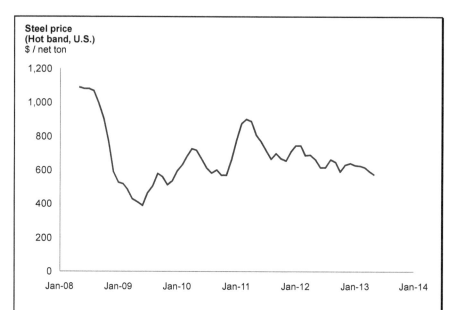

Fig. 39. Steel price development in the United States (hot band).
Source: AMM.

Probably the boldest step included significant changes to the senior management team. The prior senior management at SNA was a group of very accomplished executives who each had more than 25 or 30 years of experience in the steel industry. Being fully aware of the value of experience, I made the counter-intuitive decision to replace half of the senior leadership team with a group of people who were not accomplished steel executives or plant operators. My new leadership team had multi-disciplinary backgrounds from various industries, diverse func-tional experiences, had experience with change management, and was very di-verse. One thing, however, was common among everyone in the team: An im-mense drive to use their new responsibility to accomplish something meaningful and to make a difference for everyone in the company.

This change in senior management was a highly unconventional move for a steel company that was in existence for nearly 100 years. For many rather experienced colleagues, the changes were almost similar to a corporate earthquake. But it was not the only change that the company saw.

At the next step, we looked at a few key aspects in how we optimized our raw material use, especially at our electric-arc furnace plant in Mississippi. In simple terms, the plant took different grades of scrap metal, put it into a bucket, melted it with high-powered electricity, then poured the molten scrap into a caster and turned it into flat steel sheets. By applying knowledge from other industries, such as oil refining, it became clear that most of the value in similar processing industries came from the mix of the raw materials. With some simple changes on how to think about the raw material mix combined with the analytic horsepower to maximize the value in use of different scrap grades, we were able to increase profitability per ton of steel by nearly a factor of 3×.

As a next step, we looked at our commercial contracting exposure. Applying insights into cost curves and optimizing procurement and sales contracting exposure, we started optimizing our contracts for each asset along the respective position of the assets on the cost curve. Given the nature of the majority of our raw material contracts, this included mostly changing the mix of our sales contracts to align them with the same spot/fixed price contracting structure as the raw material contracts. Given that the electric-arc furnace plant was a low-cost asset, we remained fairly open to spot market exposure, while the integrated steel plant had a higher share of fixed price contracts given its position more towards the middle or right side of the cost curve.

The contracting approach was complemented by improvements in both our sales and procurement approaches. For example, we introduced an active approach to manage our margins per customer, and we started building more leverage against our suppliers to be able to control spending. A subsequent change in the incentive systems for procurement and sales people was put in place to provide support for aligning incentives in commercial contracting with our corporate targets. For example, the sales team was not only incentivized by volume, but also by the margin generated by each customer and contract. The procurement team was incentivized by both the price performance and operational effectiveness of their purchasing decision as well as attaining and maintaining healthy working capital levels (inventory, accounts payable).

The next change included a deliberate focus on cash preservation. When I took over, the company was generating negative cash flows on a consistent basis. While a fair share of it was due to recent capacity expansions, the company's capital structure as well as working capital approach showed potential for improvements. By refinancing our debt, optimizing inventory levels, and taking proactive steps to improve accounts receivable and accounts payable, we were able to significantly reduce the cash needs, and subsequently turned the company into an entity delivering nearly $150 million of cash per year.

Another significant change included a fundamental shift in how the company was run. Building on the insights about speed in execution, we placed a deliberate focus on making quick decisions and executing them at lightning speed. We effectively reduced the speculative element from betting on where the cycle would be the next month or next quarter, and executed on the right things with a through cycle view.

One last important thing to mention may probably be the most visible change that was introduced: A change in culture and employee engagement, driven by participation and transparency. I made it a personal goal for myself to be on the plant floor at least 1 day a week to listen to my colleagues and understand their concerns and needs. I had asked the same from my entire executive team. In addition, we started sharing information about our performance with everyone in the company; for instance, I started sharing with every employee the same dashboard that I saw every Monday morning to make decisions on how to run the company. This released a tremendous feeling of ownership and motivated everyone to give it one more push to drive up performance. Another element that helped tremendously improve engagement of the workforce was a simple idea: We started a sports competition between the different departments across both plants. This not only increased team spirit (and hopefully the physical health of the workforce!), but it also showed everyone that we are one company, one team, one culture where the CEO shared the basketball court with the hot mill janitor. Several hundred employees actively participated in those regular sports activities which were a great equalizer.

In summary, these changes that were introduced seemed to have led to good results (Figure 40). The turnaround was certainly due to improvements in the overall market conditions; however, the company's profitability jump by over 100 percent overall was in a large part driven by these changes.

The Severstal North America turnaround shows that applying the basic and fundamental concepts presented in this book can lead to superior results even within relatively short periods of time.

Saikat Dey

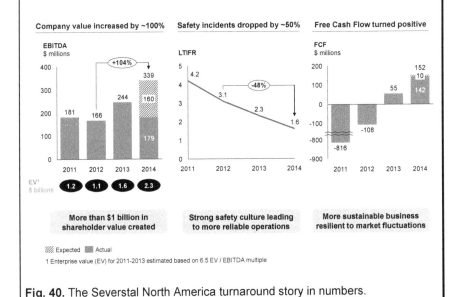

Fig. 40. The Severstal North America turnaround story in numbers.

The Severstal North America example shows that this thinking works and can be immensely successfully. However, while this seems simple, it is by no means easy. Going back to the previously described levers, an organization needs to have three key ingredients in place to pull off a successful through cycle strategy that creates value:

(1) **Internal consistency across all its functions**. Once an organization decides on what its through cycle strategy is, it has to ensure that its different functions (sales, procurement, operations, strategy, mergers and acquisitions, finance, human resources) all have to work in an internally consistent fashion. Please refer to Figure 41.

Why is internal consistency important? Let's take, for example, a company with marginal assets (assets placed on the right side of the cost curve). The company's think tank understands that its assets may not be able to weather the downside risk of volatile pricing and hence prefers long-term fixed-price contracts. However, the sales team sees it otherwise and starts putting out its volumes on the spot market. While in the short term when prices are rising, this may seem like a good idea, but when the cycle turns, the sales team may not be able

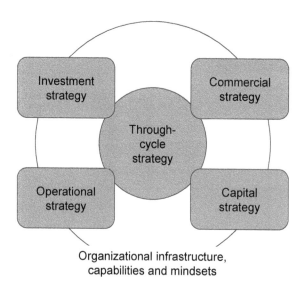

Fig. 41. An effective through cycle strategy is based on integrating multiple core functions across a company.

to convert these back into fixed pricing deals in time. This lack of internal consistency thus leads to the destruction of value and may ultimately lead to the failure of the organization. This is a critical framework and we will extensively refer to it in the next chapter.

(2) **Discipline and managerial courage**. As you can see from the example above, in cyclical markets it's very easy to lose your head. On one end of the cycle is the possibility of very high prices, attractive assets, and high cash generation, while on the other side it sometimes feels like the end of the world. The ability of the CEO and management team to keep an even keel and remain disciplined in the face of these adverse conditions is critical. Managerial courage is another attribute that cannot be stressed enough. While in the short term, this disciplined approach may seem to be value-destructive, but over the cycle this approach is what will ensure the long-term vitality and viability of the company. Often management teams, investors, and boards lose faith midway and give in to short-term comforts at the expense of longer-term returns. This is also one of the root causes why most successful companies in cyclical commodities are private or behave like one. Remaining private allows them to concentrate beyond the quarterly earnings and dividend pressures they face from the public equity markets.

(3) **Tailor decision making to organizational speed and capacity**. While most management gurus have often expressed the idea that faster is better, the more apt way to think about this is to adapt one's decision making to the execution speed that one's organization can achieve. For example, one can decide to make a divestment of an asset

within 2 months, but if the organization is unable to deliver the transaction in the given timeline, the impact can be exactly the opposite of what the intended outcome was in the first place. It is often the case that most organizations cannot execute fast enough to changes in the cycle. At that time it is more appropriate to adopt a consistent and disciplined approach and stick to it irrespective of the current state of the cycle.

To summarize this chapter, we covered the following:

- Managing a cycle needs to be internally consistent and integrated.
- Discipline and managerial courage are important attributes to ensuring resilience through the cycle.
- Decision making must take into account the organization's capability to execute in a timely fashion.

While we have learned in this chapter how all concepts can fit together into one coherent cycle management approach including the real-world example of the successful turnaround of the steel company Severstal North America, the next chapter will explain the primary archetypes of the presented framework that are typically adopted by successful commodity companies.

VII. The Three Winning Archetypes

While there is no one size fits all in terms of the models that companies can adopt to beat cycles, there are, however, three primary archetypes that seem to consistently perform better than others for companies in the same industry (Figure 42). The three archetypes that will be explained in more detail below are the following:

- Non-conformer
- Shaper
- Timer

As one can see from Figure 42, each player has unique defining characteristics that we will discuss in detail shortly, but they all share some common attributes which are table stakes for any player looking to out-perform across the cycle:

- **Strong balance sheet**. Players are unafraid to build a stockpile of capital against investor pressure to dividend them out or make expensive acquisitions.
- **Decision making tailored to organizational capability to execute**. Management teams design a through cycle strategy that takes into account the organization's capability to execute and deliver.

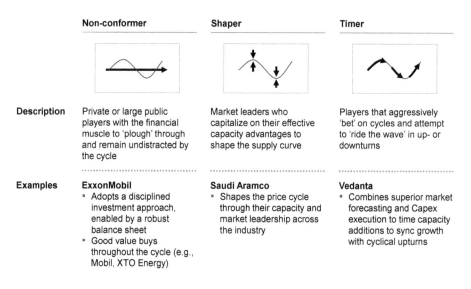

	Non-conformer	Shaper	Timer
Description	Private or large public players with the financial muscle to 'plough' through and remain undistracted by the cycle	Market leaders who capitalize on their effective capacity advantages to shape the supply curve	Players that aggressively 'bet' on cycles and attempt to 'ride the wave' in up- or downturns
Examples	**ExxonMobil** ▪ Adopts a disciplined investment approach, enabled by a robust balance sheet ▪ Good value buys throughout the cycle (e.g., Mobil, XTO Energy)	**Saudi Aramco** ▪ Shapes the price cycle through their capacity and market leadership across the industry	**Vedanta** ▪ Combines superior market forecasting and Capex execution to time capacity additions to sync growth with cyclical upturns

Fig. 42. Three winning archetypes for creating value across cycles.

- **Small decision making teams**. The cerebral part of decision making is not spread out across too many players, layers, or people; but it is limited to a small team.

- **Behavior like a private company**. The company is not distracted by the pressures of the public equity markets and it makes decisions with a longer investment horizon.

- **Internally consistent strategy and disciplined execution**. All aspects of the strategy to navigate the cycle resonate and the organization is disciplined in its execution. Becoming distracted or losing one's nerves in the face of the cycle is not tolerated.

Beyond the table stake characteristics mentioned above, each archetype demonstrates a few unique hallmarks. Let's analyze each in more detail in the following paragraphs.

Non–conformers: Plow Through the Cycle

Non-conformers typically demonstrate the fortitude and discipline to "plow" through the cycle. This archetype's defining character trait is its consistent investment philosophy which remains unchanged across the cycle. Consider the graphic in Figure 43.

When you compare ExxonMobil versus the other two major oil and gas producers, Shell and BP, you notice a distinct difference in how Exxon invests across the cycle. Exxon seems to be investing evenly across the cycle while building up massive cash reserves. On the other hand, Shell and BP seem to invest in line with crude prices. As crude prices rise, Shell and BP increase their capital investments and reduce their capital outlays when the price of crude is

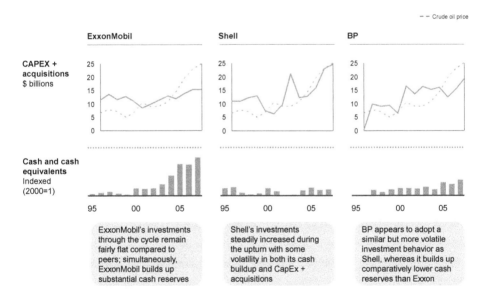

Fig. 43. Approaches to the cycle: A comparison of the three major oil and gas producers.

Source: Company 10-K, team analysis.

falling. Both, however, seem to fail in building up the same level of cash reserves as Exxon across the cycle. There are two primary reasons for this:

(1) Exxon's investment philosophy is based on its underlying assumption of the long-term equilibrium value of crude rather than what the prevailing price of crude is at that time. This allows Exxon to pass on overpriced assets at the top of the cycle and pick up "crown jewels" at the bottom of the cycle. Doing this effectively across the cycle ensures that they pay a lot less for their acquisitions across the cycle and end up with a far superior set of assets, especially during cyclical downturns.

(2) Exxon ensures that its production assets remain fully exposed to the cycle. In fact, it is surprising to note that it is very difficult to get a long-term fixed price from Exxon on most commodities that they produce which happen to be some of the most widely traded commodities on the futures market (e.g., natural gas, gasoline, refined products, crude oil). This ensures that these low-cost assets generate the highest returns across a cycle, with the intrinsic volatility being something that Exxon seems to welcome rather than shy away from. Their competitors, however, offer long-term fixed-price contracts and place significant volumes through these contracts, effectively passing up on the upside from cyclical peaks when they happen.

The combination of the two factors above in conjunction with the discipline of not being distracted from the long-term equilibrium price of crude or the relevant commodity is what makes Exxon and other non-conformers so formidable.

Shapers: Shape the Cycle

Shapers are players who capitalize on their overall share of capacity on the cost curve to actually modulate its shape and determine the marginal producer, and resultantly the market price and margins for the entire industry. They effectively shape the cycle itself. However, in order to shape the cycle, there are three critical conditions that need to be fulfilled:

(1) **Ability**. Does the individual player have the ability to modulate the cost curve to determine who the marginal producer is? Please consider the graph in Figure 44.

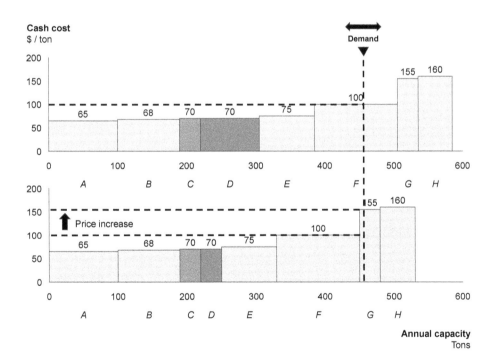

Fig. 44. A cost curve situation explaining a company's ability to be a "shaper."

In the example, you can see a steep shoulder in the cost curve. If the industry can cut back supply by around 60 tons of production volume, then G becomes the marginal producer and prices can rise by over $50/ton. Let's consider the two players C and D highlighted in Figure 44. Can they unilaterally and without cooperation with anyone else cause a change in the marginal producer from F to G? The answer in the case of D is "Yes" but in the case of C it is "No." The reason is that C would need to shut down all its capacity and more in order to make G the marginal producer. This proves the point that the ability to be able to influence the cost curve—while not violating anti-trust concerns—is one of the founding blocks of being a "shaper."

(2) **Incentive**. The next question to ask is: Does the individual player have the incentive to curtail capacity? Let's revisit the same graphic in Figure 44 and focus on the player D, the one we determined having the ability to curtail capacity on the cost curve (see Figure 45).

In the first case, the total margin made by producer D is "x," while in the second case after curtailing production by over 60 tons the total margin made by D is "y." However, D is only incentivized to cut production if y > x, which means the total profit made in the second scenario far outweighs the first. In some other cases, a company will cut back capacity to accommodate a new entrant and to ensure that the high cost marginal producer stays afloat. In this case, it is the case of potentially lower margins that is tallied up against the scenario of holding prices steady at lesser production volumes.

(3) **Behavior**. The last critical factor for a player's ability to shape the cost curve is an external factor, which is the expected behavior of the rest of the players. Assuming producer D had both the ability and the

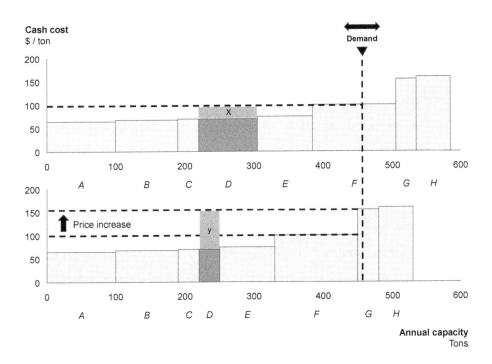

Fig. 45. The cost curve situation explaining a company's incentive to be a "shaper."

incentive to reduce production and goes ahead with it, would producer *A* see this as an opportunity to increase capacity and take away
market share from *D*? This would be very detrimental as this would
mean that the marginal producer would still remain *F* and effectively
keep prices low for the industry. Player *D* would see this as a wasted
move on its part and would try and claw back market share from others through discounting. It is at this time that the entire industry falls
into a prolonged period of below marginal producer pricing, effectively shutting down these producers and reducing overall margins
for the industry.

One example of a company that has applied the strategy of being a shaper very effectively can be found in the commodity chemicals industry. The company—in the following referred to as ChemCo—has effectively used its capacity leadership and intimate knowledge of demand trends to effectively navigate the cycle. The company's ability to shape extends from their extensive logistics, ships and port networks across the globe, which makes them touch the overwhelming majority of these molecules being traded in the world. This provided them with early knowledge of demand trends on a global basis, helping them position capacity effectively on the cost curve. And while they did not own more than 15 percent of the direct market share, their innovative use of capacity swaps and offtake agreements with their own competitors ensured that they had all three criteria to shape in place—ability, incentive, and industry behavior. So the

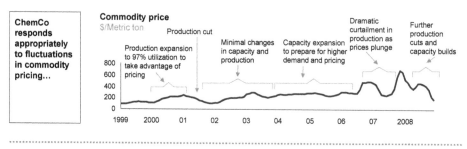

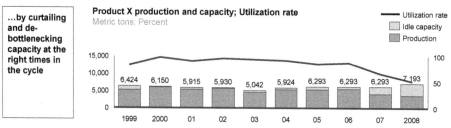

Fig. 46. Capacity leadership allowed ChemCo to effectively manage capacity for product X.

ability to influence supply coupled with a global understanding of demand trends through their extensive logistics network ensured that this company was able to modulate capacity on the cost curve. Figure 46 shows over a 10-year period how ChemCo effectively managed capacity by appropriately responding to fluctuations in commodity pricing.

In conclusion, shapers need an industry which is well-behaved and has good conduct. This is usually achieved when the individuals in the industry understand the concepts outlined above or when one of the producers has enough flexing capacity within its assets that it can punitively punish the bad behavior of other players by putting them out of the money on the cost curve.

Timers: Aggressively Bet On the Cycle

Timers are characterized by players who aggressively "bet" on cycles and attempt to "ride the wave" in up- or downturns. They have to base their entire strategy on their ability to read the cycle better than everyone else and "bet" on that information. This is usually achieved through a combination of commercial contracting, ability to execute projects faster than their competition, and well-timed acquisitions or divestitures.

One example of a timer who has demonstrated the ability to do so consistently is Vedanta from the mining industry. For the broader part of the last decade, Vedanta consistently demonstrated the ability to execute projects and time their commissioning at the right time before the peak of the cycle for most of their projects. Their superior execution of capital projects and the ability to time it optimally to cyclical peaks ensured value generation that far exceeded their competition as shown in Figure 47.

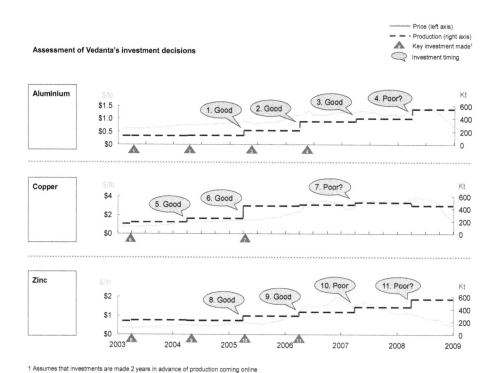

Fig. 47. Vedanta is an example of a company that successfully adopted to being a "timer."
Source: Company filings, Datastream, team analysis.

In addition, Vedanta's ability to execute projects at a fraction of the cost of their competition is another key highlight to their competitive advantage as demonstrated in Figure 48. While the broad majority of their projects were executed in India in the first half of the decade, this advantage may have eroded over time as they rapidly expanded beyond India.

Usually, organizations that are nimble and can move fast are best suited to adopt this "timer" archetype. This strategy is intrinsically more risky. Sustaining the strategy over multiple cycles is often the test that distinguishes the winners.

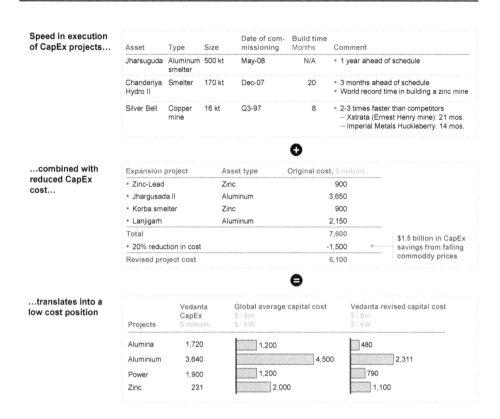

Fig. 48. Vedanta's ability to execute capital projects quickly.

Source: Vedanta investor presentations, Vedanta annual reports, team analysis.

More people fail at this than succeed and most companies that become significantly sizeable through timing need to quickly adapt to another archetype to ensure their long-term survival. Another classic example of a good timer is Mittal Steel which grew from having one plant in Trinidad to buying Arcelor (at that time the largest steelmaker in the world) through a series of well-timed acquisitions.

As companies look towards potentially adopting a through cycle philosophy they need to ask themselves questions along the following lines, as shown in the logic tree exhibit in Figure 49:

(1) Do you have the ability, incentive, and industry behavior that will allow you to shape the industry? If yes, adopt the "shaper" archetype.
If no, then answer question 2 below.

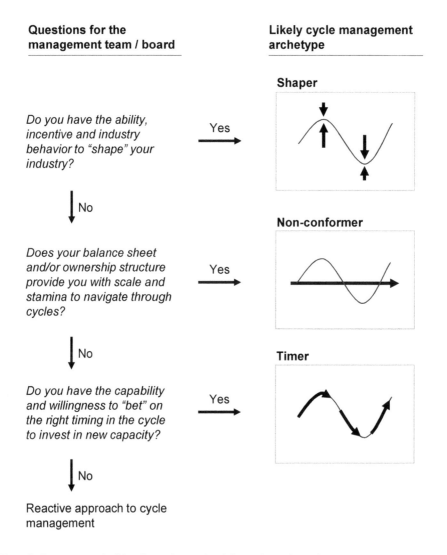

Fig. 49. Process to decide about the optimal through cycle archetype.

(2) Does your balance sheet or ownership structure provide you with the scale, discipline, and stamina to plow through the cycle? If yes, then pursue a "non- conformer" archetype; if no, then answer question 3.

(3) Do you have the capability and willingness to "bet" on the cycle? If yes, adopt a "timer" archetype, and if no, then try and change some of the parameters mentioned in questions 1 to 3, or else you are likely to be subject to becoming a reactive player and your best option at that point may be to find a good valuation for your assets to get out.

To summarize this chapter, it's important to note that:

- We have observed three primary archetypes that win across the cycle, namely non-conformers, shapers, and timers.

- While all three share a lot of common underlying characteristics, they each have their defining attributes.

- For a non-conformer, it's the ability to remain undistracted by the cycle and plow through the cycle with a disciplined investment and commercial process.

- For a shaper, it's the ability to flex their production capacities across the cost curve to determine the marginal producer.

- For a timer, it's their ability to "call the cycle" better than others and aggressively making bets on the same to outperform their competitors. However, this is a risky proposition and is usually difficult to sustain.

- And finally, utilize a simple framework to determine which archetype suits you the best and stick with it. Disciplined execution is key to a successful outcome.

This chapter has concluded the insights of this book by providing three archetypes that executives can adopt to win in cyclical commodity markets. The next chapter will look ahead and talk about how this knowledge can be used going forward.

VIII. Applying the Insights of this Book

If you have made it to this chapter, congratulations! We have come very far and are about to close this book with some concluding thoughts. Before we get there, let's recap what we learned so far:

- We learned what makes cyclical commodity markets tick and how they are different from other industries.
- We understand the most powerful tool that can be used in any commodity market: The cost curve.
- We know how to apply the cost curve in a real-world context to draw meaningful conclusions.
- We understand what cycles are, how they happen, and why they exist, especially in commodity markets.
- We learned about the Top Ten things that successful companies do differently than average performers in cyclical markets, most of them being counter-intuitive to common belief and conventional wisdom.
- We understand how everything can be put together in a simple framework that can be used to improve performance in any commodity market along five levers: organizational fabric, investment strategy, commercial strategy, capital strategy, and operational strategy.

- We have seen how the framework has been successfully applied in a real-world example: The turnaround of the steel producer Severstal North America.

- We understand what archetypes companies can choose going forward to improve their through cycle management strategy.

Taking all the insights into account that come along with the points mentioned above, one additional insight that has been touched upon multiple times throughout the book deals with talent. Its importance cannot be under-estimated, because all of the required changes and strategies described can only be made possible with the right people. As pointed out multiple times throughout the book, a lot of the insights have to do with the mindset of the leadership which is responsible for making the investment, commercial, capital, and operational decisions in the organization. Existing mindsets will deliver existing results. If you want different results, you need to have different mindsets. Especially if you want your company to be attractive to young engineering and management talent, your company culture needs to be open for this new talent. Large cohorts of young talent is nowadays starting with companies that are known for an open, transparent, and meritocratic culture, such as the likes of Google, Facebook, McKinsey, or Amazon. While it would be false to attempt to attract the same talent with the same methods, such as Google, commodity companies need to find their own way of hiring young and aspiring talent. A few ways how it can be done have been mentioned in this book already; the main concepts to attract talent deal with transparency, career progression, and meritocracy. Good talent wants to see that they can have an impact. Young talent also needs to know that they can become successful even at relatively younger ages. Meritocracy should be more important than seniority. If those points are considered and adopted, the rest will fall into place much easier.

At this stage of the book, you might ask yourself: Okay, I get that, but why is all of this important? Our answer is simple: Because many, if not all of the introduced concepts are applicable in many different contexts. While the book has been written with cyclical commodity markets in mind, the basic fundamentals behind each of the presented insights are equally applicable in other industries and sectors alike, because they are based on fundamental economic principles that hold true in any context or environment. Certainly, the extent to which the applicability is relevant in other areas might change from industry to industry or from sector to sector; however, the main takeaways are similar. For instance, supply in any industry is based on the concept of a cost curve; that means companies are producing their products at different costs. Pricing in any industry is set at the intersection of demand and supply, whereas demand and supply are never constant and might change frequently; perhaps not as frequently or with the same intensity as in the case of commodity industries, but at least to a certain degree.

Industries or sectors that can particularly benefit from the insights offered in this book are industries that face similar characteristics to commodity markets. This can include transport and logistics, infrastructure, real estate, semi-conductors, or many other industrial manufacturing industries. Beyond that, the concepts of this book can also be applied in other areas, such as principal investing or equity research, particularly by analysts who cover companies in cyclical commodity markets.

In terms of functional areas, the book is relevant to any general management function—most particularly to senior management who is responsible for making most of the decisions raised in this book. However, middle management and especially younger talent is encouraged to learn from this book as well. At the end of the day, this book has one central message: Help managers and investors adopt a different mindset about how they think of commodity markets. The fact that most of the insights in this book are counter-intuitive to widely applied practices implies that the book is mostly about a change in mindset, and to a lesser extent, about changes in capabilities, methods, or tools.

If this book helps current or future leaders embrace the excitement of commodity markets and enables them to adopt a new mindset on how to think about commodity markets, we believe the book has accomplished its mission. At the end of the day, managing through commodity markets is the application of basic economics combined with common sense execution. You will know that you understand the entire concept of this book when you understand that "creating value within commodities is simple, but not easy" (as adopted from Warren Buffett).

To learn more about how to manage through cyclical commodity markets, please visit the following website: www.uncommoditized.com.

Index